Timber Frame
Hybrids

Timber Frame *Hybrids*

Enduring Traditions, Boundless Possibilities

Anthony F. Zaya
and Tim Diener

4880 Lower Valley Road, Atglen, Pennsylvania 19310

Opposite page:

Lancaster County Timber Frames, Inc. custom designs and hand crafts timber frames. The company has designed, carved, and erected frames in twenty states – from Vermont to Tennessee, Massachusetts to New Mexico. Their work has received numerous local, state, national, and international awards, and has been featured on the covers of a dozen magazines. One of their projects was recently selected by the HGTV channel for its season-long "Dream House" series, tentatively scheduled for broadcast during the 2008 season. In 2007 Lancaster County Timber Frames, Inc. was named to the Inc.5000 list of the fastest growing private companies in America. www.lancotf.com

Other Schiffer Books on Related Subjects
Artisan Crafted Timber Frame Homes. Tina Skinner.
Authentic Log Homes Restored: Timbers for Today's Homesteads. Ferris Robbinson.
Barn-style Homes: Design Ideas for Timber Frame Houses. Tina Skinner and Tony Hanslin.
Cedar Homes. Tina Skinner.
Half-Timber Architecture. Tina Skinner.
Living Barns: How to Find and Restore a Barn of Your Own. Ernest Burden.
Log & Timber Frame Homes. Tina Skinner.
Old Barns - New Homes: A Showcase of Architectural Conversions. E. Ashley Rooncy.
Room by Room by Room. Tina Skinner and Tony Hanslin.

Copyright © 2008 by Anthony F. Zaya and Tim Diener
Library of Congress Control Number: 2007941587

All rights reserved. No part of this work may be reproduced or used in any fwhout written permission from the publisher.
The scanning, uploading and distribution of this book or any part thereof via the Internet or via any other means without the permission of the publisher is illegal and punishable by law. Please purchase only authorized editions and do not participate in or encourage the electronic piracy of copyrighted materials.
"Schiffer," "Schiffer Publishing Ltd. & Design," and the "Design of pen and ink well" are registered trademarks of Schiffer Publishing Ltd.

Designed by "Sue"
Type set in Bernhard Modern BT/Aldine 721 BT

ISBN: 978-0-7643-2894-7
Printed in China

Schiffer Books are available at special discounts for bulk purchases for sales promotions or premiums. Special editions, including personalized covers, corporate imprints, and excerpts can be created in large quantities for special needs. For more information contact the publisher:

Published by Schiffer Publishing Ltd.
4880 Lower Valley Road
Atglen, PA 19310
Phone: (610) 593-1777; Fax: (610) 593-2002
E-mail: Info@schifferbooks.com

For the largest selection of fine reference books on this and related subjects, please visit our web site at **www.schiffer-books.com**
We are always looking for people to write books on new and related subjects. If you have an idea for a book please contact us at the above address.

This book may be purchased from the publisher.
Include $3.95 for shipping.
Please try your bookstore first.
You may write for a free catalog.

In Europe, Schiffer books are distributed by
Bushwood Books
6 Marksbury Ave.
Kew Gardens
Surrey TW9 4JF England
Phone: 44 (0) 20 8392-8585; Fax: 44 (0) 20 8392-9876
E-mail: info@bushwoodbooks.co.uk
Website: www.bushwoodbooks.co.uk
Free postage in the U.K., Europe; air mail at cost.

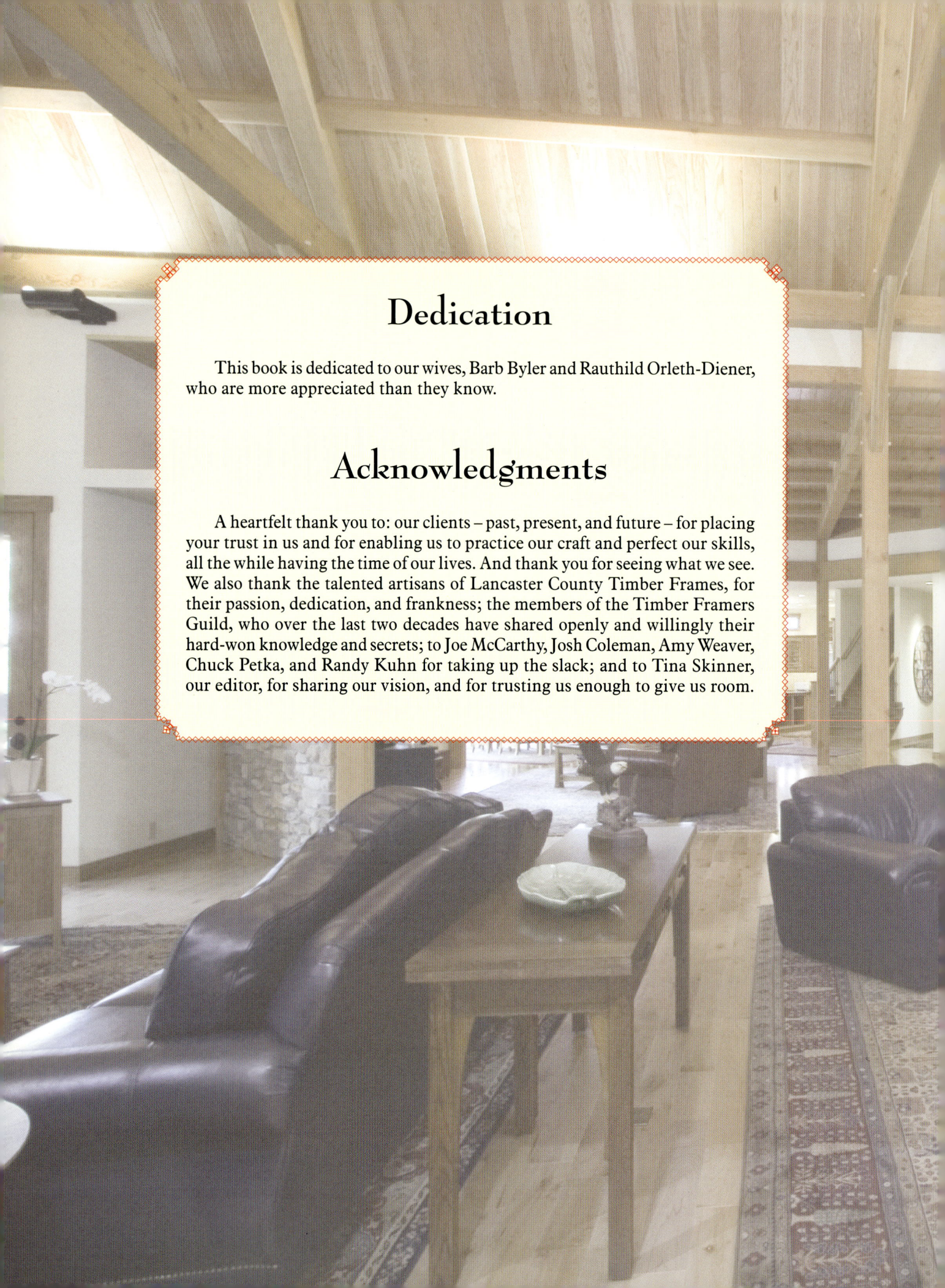

Dedication

This book is dedicated to our wives, Barb Byler and Rauthild Orleth-Diener, who are more appreciated than they know.

Acknowledgments

A heartfelt thank you to: our clients – past, present, and future – for placing your trust in us and for enabling us to practice our craft and perfect our skills, all the while having the time of our lives. And thank you for seeing what we see. We also thank the talented artisans of Lancaster County Timber Frames, for their passion, dedication, and frankness; the members of the Timber Framers Guild, who over the last two decades have shared openly and willingly their hard-won knowledge and secrets; to Joe McCarthy, Josh Coleman, Amy Weaver, Chuck Petka, and Randy Kuhn for taking up the slack; and to Tina Skinner, our editor, for sharing our vision, and for trusting us enough to give us room.

CONTENTS

Acknowledgments 6
Foreword 8
The Heart of the Matter 9
A History of Timber Frame Hybrids 10
   An Appreciation of Timber Framing 10
   Earliest Beginnings 11
   Far-Eastern Beginnings 15
   Timber Construction in the West – the Mediterranean 20
   Rome: Utilitas – firmitas – venustas 23
   Northern Europe in the Middle Ages and Renaissance 25
   Timber Construction on American Soil 29
   The American Revival 31
The Case for Hybrid Timber Frames 33
The Range of Choices 35
A Gallery of Timber Frame Hybrids 45
Making it Work 136
   Hybrid Timber Frames and Truss Work 136
   Flat Ceilings 139
   Completing the Roof 142
The Process 145
Additional Considerations 152
A Final Note 158
Postscript 159
Bibliography 160

FOREWORD

Imagination is everything. It's the preview of life's coming attractions.
—Albert Einstein

Two decades after I'd last been at my grandfather's house as a child, and several years after his passing, my mother and I discovered a forgotten box stashed in a closet at home. We opened it together. One of the items inside was an embroidered pillow that I immediately pressed to my face. I drew in a big whiff and was quickly pulled back in time to grandpa's elegant home.

Olfactory recollection – it's a powerful transporter beam. It's that moment of being moved, as long-forgotten smells from an old, familiar place are reintroduced, when many of us experience remarkable clarity of something from our past, an emotion, insight, warmth, even tears.

For me, stepping into a barn produces the same effect, though the experience is always good. The smell surrounds and accentuates what's there. But it is the building's organic, skeletal form, seen from inside, that adds the most powerful dimension. We see, and with a sense of wonder appreciate, the elegant simplicity of it. Like the timbers, joined together by thinking minds and skilled hands, we too are connected to it, pulled in.

And this is what makes even new timbered structures so appealing to most of us. Being in them is a dimensional experience, with facets that aren't present when we're surrounded by squared walls and ceilings and flat surfaces. In a timber frame, we become a part of that space. And it, in turn, gives something unique to each of us.

What's especially appealing is a sense of appreciation for the skill – and even more importantly, the *imagination* – of the people who planned and sculpted it. After all, they designed it to draw you in, to romance you with its form and warmth and personality.

Einstein had it right. For the timber framer, each new work is an imaginative expression that plays the senses and is a preview of coming attractions.

You're lying on your back in the forest, gazing upwards as you take in the cathedral's arched space above, where branches reach out, intermingle, and support the sky. A fine frame will give you that sense of fascination.

And surely, Einstein would have appreciated its mathematical precision because, after all, each frame design is a blend of math and art, a formula, with each piece engineered to fit in just so. Its dual purpose is to work structurally and aesthetically. A fine frame will go even further, enticing you with its balance, warmth, and charm.

I recall my first *intelligent* encounter with a timber frame. The year was 1999. My wife Erika and I were contemplating the possibility of a new timber frame home. The first frame we visited was pure beauty. The voice that floated through the forest of timbers was deep and resonant – a memorable part of the experience. When you speak with Tony Zaya, you're not likely to forget it, either.

During that day, while visiting several projects they'd completed and the facility where their crews were working on frames for other customers, we were educated. We learned things about timber framing that I thought would be impossible to communicate in the written form. Until, that is, Tony and Tim Diener shared this superbly detailed and illustrated manuscript for this book with me. I was delighted that they asked me to review it and to offer this introduction for you.

My eager participation is simply an extension of that first day with Tony, our first impression of the firm, and – now – an enduring romance with timber frames. We knew that our very first exploration was a rare encounter. Just prior to building the home we now live in, we'd immediately found the craftsman and the company to work with. And unexpectedly we'd found friendship and wise counsel in Tony.

Ultimately, we settled on a plan to do timber framing in the great room; the space is unique and inviting. With arched hammer beams and a queenposts on the far wall, purlins that join them and knotty pine ceiling – it's a room we've come to love. A few years later, needing more of that woody experience (and the excitement of construction), Lancaster County Timber Frames designed and built a timbered porch for the front of our home.

We've since come to know many of the artisans at Lancaster County Timber Frames and have great appreciation for their dedication to the craft. Among them is Tim Diener, whose additional abilities as a writer, photographer, and historian have added substantially to the talent pool there.

Think back to your earliest encounter with a timbered structure. That first impression, whether simple or complex, *is* a preview of things to come. Because, no matter how many times you've seen or experienced it, there's always more there, more to it, more to be discovered and enjoyed. I'm sure you'll enjoy, and treasure, *Timber Frame Hybrids*.

—John Vastyan, President
Common Ground

THE HEART OF THE MATTER

Of the more than twenty years in which I have practiced this fascinating craft of timber framing, the first five or so were spent designing, carving, and erecting what can probably be called "whole house" timber frames. The thought of timber framing only one room or even several areas of a house, unless the project was an addition to an existing house, never held any interest for me. In fact, back then I probably would have considered the very idea blasphemous. Timber framing was such a noble method of construction that I saw no reason not to do it everywhere. At that time most of my colleagues and competitors were pretty much of the same mindset.

Then I met a woman who shook me out of my haze. She wanted to design and build a new home. It was to be rather large and finely detailed. She wanted to incorporate timber framing, but only in the ceiling of her great room. I tried, in my very subtle style, to convince her that if a little bit of timber framing is good, why not use a lot of it. Her response – "I see no need to use good timbers where they are not needed, or won't be seen, or where they'll complicate matters. Besides, I don't want to tire of it" – had an effect on me. In fact, it was the seed of this book, and I've since married her.

Of all the material on this planet, wood is the most beloved. The veracity of this statement can be supported if one puts any weight on the proposition that "imitation is the sincerest form of flattery." For no other material has been mimicked as long, as constantly, and as often as wood. For thousands of years we have tried to capture the look and texture of wood and the construction details appropriate to it in order to imbue other materials with its essence – first in stone, then plaster and concrete, then aluminum and plastics. But none has ever captured its soul.

During the 1960s, a company marketed, rather successfully, a urethane product with a U-shaped cross section and an exterior surface that copied the look and color of dark, hand hewn timbers, ostensibly taken from an old timber framed barn. There were even indications of pegs embossed along the length. The imitations, available in several dimensions and lengths, were intended to be glued to ceilings and even sidewalls. Though probably well intended, it was a flawed attempt to imbue our homes with something that had been missing for generations – the feeling of strength and warmth and permanence that only heavy timbers, intricately joined, can yield. It was a sorry attempt, more a caricature than a facsimile. The installed arrangement of these plastic timbers most often defied any sense of logic or intuitive engineering. For a material to impart a sense of integrity, it must be real, size appropriate, and the geometry involved must make sense. A weightless foam 6" x 8" beam, spanning 32 feet and showing maybe three butt joints, gets everything wrong.

I had assumed that such nonsense ceased decades ago. A recent journey through cyberspace shows otherwise; a number of companies have resurrected this zombie – just in a more varied form. Now you can buy not only foam beams of varying sizes, but also corbels and braces of varying shapes, as well as "rubber beam strapping to replicate that look of fastening hardware." How desperate are we for a sense of permanence and substance? If this is flattery then what is insult?

Perhaps most interesting is that, to the very best of my knowledge, I have never encountered a situation where wood mimicked any other material. It must be that wood, unlike other materials (except stone and glass), is comfortable in its own skin – and for good reason. It is stronger pound for pound than steel, and in heavy timber sizes it retains its structural integrity in a fire much longer than steel. Moreover, production of steel, glass, and concrete requires approximately 24, 14, and 6 times more energy, respectively, than does wood to make a final product. Yet, wood is friendly. It has warmth and beauty. It invites touching. It is organic; it once had life, and, during that life it supplied us with oxygen. It is reusable and biodegradable. It is the only renewable structural building material we have. It is virtually infinite in its variety. Each piece, each timber is singular; no two pieces are the same, much like we humans.

—A.F. Zaya

A HISTORY OF TIMBER CONSTRUCTION

An Appreciation of Timber Framing

Anyone stepping into a timber-framed home for the first time cannot help but be struck by the unabashed forcefulness, the frankly utilitarian ethos, the often stark functionality of the timbered structure. We stand awed by the massive timbers methodically knit together into a skeleton for the sheltering envelope. Instinctively, we pay tactile homage to the framework, caressing the timbers, absorbing their warmth and vigor by running our hands over oiled, smooth or hand-hewn faces, playing our fingers over chamfered edges, testing our knuckles against the timbers' solidity to confirm what our eyes and fingers have told us. Our eyes, in turn, follow the contours of the timber beams and playfully retrace the responses of the timberwright to the need for more support here, some bracing there; they probe the timber joinery and linger over the patterns of pegs. The senses delight in the shear physicality of the framework, in the sculpted penetrating masses, in the interplay of volume and mass, lightness and weight, openness and spatial definition.

Language captures but a fragment of this experience. This isn't surprising, for in this encounter what the senses are engaged in is older than language itself: the elemental experience of shelter, of dwelling, needing only the simplest tools the senses provide. It is an encounter with the timeless. Shop-worn though it may be, the notion of the timelessness of timber framing is a serviceable enough starting point for a history of the timber frame hybrid. For when the appraising eye, fingers, hands, and knuckles make their first acquaintance with the heavy beams of a timber frame, they are re-enacting the early human's own need to explore the worthiness of his dwelling, expressing their appreciation of a shelter well-formed.

Timber framing is the art and craft – science, some might say – of connecting heavy timbers using various kinds of mortise and tenon joinery to form a structural framework. In those parts of the world blessed with the necessary resources it has been one of the dominant construction methods for over two thousand years. And for close to seven thousand years, timber framing of one description or another has been continuously practiced. The *evolutionary* history of timber framing, however, stretches back to humankind's emergence from the caves. Man has been fashioning shelter with wood for so long that it is likely hard-wired into our brains. On a primal level, just as predictably as we associate bared fangs with danger, we associate timbers with strength, permanence, and shelter.

An old stone arch leads into a contemporary timber-framed kitchen.

Earliest Beginnings

Homo habilis, the first of the hominids known to have used tools fashioned from stone, is believed to have constructed the first manmade structures some two million years ago in East Africa, dwellings thought to have consisted of stones anchoring over-arching saplings to form an umbrella-shaped shelter. Similar sites have been excavated in other parts of the world, such as the Terra Amata site near Nice in the south of France, where evidence of stone-anchored wooden dwellings can be dated to a period from 500,000 to 380,000 years ago. Amazingly, the basic design of such dwellings may well have remained largely unchanged for close to a million years, encompassing both the appearance of several hominid species and vast geographical areas. In Dolni Vestonice, Czechoslovakia, archaeological excavations have unearthed a large seasonal encampment inhabited by mammoth hunters and dating to 27,000 to 23,000 years ago. Clear evidence exists here of a timbered roof structure built upon a foundation of packed clay, stone, and mammoth bones.

When and where wood was available, it was pressed into service, along with other materials, in the creation of shelter. The early examples of heavy timber most likely involved connections that were lashed together with vines, or simply relied on gravity to hold the framework together. *Timber framing* in the modern sense of the term, though, was still waiting thousands of years downstream.

We define timber framing as the art and science of creating an interconnected framework of timbers, relying on its individual members for its strength and cohesion, and on the interdependent connection of those timbers.

Given this definition, it is clear that the transition from primitive construction methods to the elegance and ingenuity of timber framing must have awaited a confluence of a great many changes in mankind's condition.

Technologically, socially, and economically, the conditions that would spur the innovative spirit and drive of mankind had to converge at specific points and places in history. Nomadic groups of hunter-gatherers could have had little use for the permanence and stability of timber-framed structures. All the ingenuity and inventive energy of the hunter-gatherer would be expended in maintaining his advantage in the hunt, and in preserving the mobility vital to his means of sustenance. Clearly, this was not the time to commit to the quest for permanence. So it was, too, with the early pastoralists. These societies had drawn the hunt into the ambit of human management, transferring the gathering activities of their hunter-gatherer kin to the herds that they tended and guided from wintering grounds to summering grounds and back. The later transition to agrarian societies tamed the peregrine nature of human communities. Much of the technological progress of agrarianism sought to tighten man's tenuous grasp on the environment.

Early hominid shelter of bound saplings.

Paleolithic timber post and animal skin shelter.

Yet even with shift from the early hunter-gather to the pastoralist and then to agrarian societies, the inspiration for the first mortise and tenon joint – and the leap forward to true timber framing – had to spring from somewhere.

Epoch-making innovation is an enigma. Where and how revolutionary progress can occur is seldom – if ever – completely accessible to the mind, rarely even with the benefit of hindsight. This might be because our minds are bound by the paradigms of our times – the system of beliefs and assumptions that hold sway over our minds. In the modern period, however, innovation has occurred at a precipitous pace. Within hardly a century, man has flown for the first time, heard voices crackling through an earpiece, conquered vast territories, and fought bitter wars with the repeating rifle; even more recently, the power of the atom has been unleashed to devastating effect; vaccines have been developed, liberating us from diseases that have beset humanity from time immemorial; the invention of the transistor has contributed to the dissolution of the boundaries of space and time.

We've become so accustomed to the vertiginous pace of innovation and change that our ability to appreciate the profound impact of slow, incremental but nonetheless earth-shaking change has dulled. Where did this inspiration spring from?

Shelter of interlocking mammoth jaws.

A naturally occurring fork or crotch in a timber post would have made a stronger joint than one simply lashed, and perhaps lacking a member so fortuitously formed, some tribe of builders lost in the mists of time simply decided to fashion their own substitute. Since time immemorial mankind had known the tough web of integument and bone that made up the skeletal structure of his prey, and even of his own anatomy. Indeed, many a Paleolithic dwelling had relied on the remains of animal prey – the bones, the skins – for structure and enclosure. The remains of primitive shelters found at the Dolni Vestonice archeological site are clear evidence of early mankind's ability to combine diverse building materials in a single structure – in a word, of a hybrid method of building! In any event, it is likely that nature supplied the inspiration for the first mortise and tenon joint. Carving interlocking joinery had to wait for the right social and technological conditions, but assembling a hut of interlocking mammoth jaws and sheathing it with animal hides already suggested the possibility some 20,000 years before.

The mortise and tenon was a revolutionary technological development of a magnitude comparable to the invention of the wheel. This is demonstrated by the breadth of technologies and cultural institutions indebted to it. The new technology of joining wood and other materials made possible the rapid advancement of not only the building of permanent dwellings, temples, and public structures, but furniture making and shipbuilding.

Many writers have assumed that the development of timber joinery followed the availability of metal tools capable of efficiently forming close-fitting wood joints. Historical evidence of timbers fashioned with stone tools suggests that the converse is more probable: the desire of our Neolithic ancestors to create structures of superior permanence and strength helped to drive the search for better tools. As mankind emerged from the late Stone Age, the mortise and tenon was already entrenched in virtually every area of material culture and technology. So fertile is the basic principle of keyed penetration at the heart of the mortise and tenon that it is still finding novel applications today.

Who inaugurated this broad trajectory, and when? Predictably, western scholarship has pointed to Mesopotamian and Egyptian civilizations. A funerary ship from circa 2,600 B.C.E. has been found that used mortised and tenoned hull construction, variations of which are found throughout sea-faring Mediterranean societies of this era. Even at this early date the already fully evolved mortise and tenon joinery used in shipbuilding and furniture making suggests earlier origins. The construction of dwellings and sacral architecture in Egypt, however, did not rely on the methods of timber joinery, and timbers were largely relegated to a role secondary to, or imitative of, stone. Stone, in its turn, often imitated other materials, such as the papyrus thought to have been the building material of pre-historic Egypt.

Egyptian temple with papyrus-inspired columns.

Far-Eastern Antecedents

Far earlier evidence of well-developed mortise and tenon joinery comes from an entirely different point on the compass – from ancient China. Archaeological exploration at the Hemudu site in the Zhejiang Province, south of the modern-day port city of Shanghai, has unearthed settlements with dwellings and other structures using extensive and sophisticated timber construction, including mortise and tenon joinery, dating to 5,000 B.C.E. The scope and magnitude of mortise and tenon joinery at this site suggests even earlier origins. By the end of the Neolithic period in China, around 2,000 B.C.E., timber joinery had completely supplanted older methods of construction which relied on lashing or binding with ropes and vines. The Chinese timber-framed house of the Neolithic period set a course that meandered through China's millennia-long history.

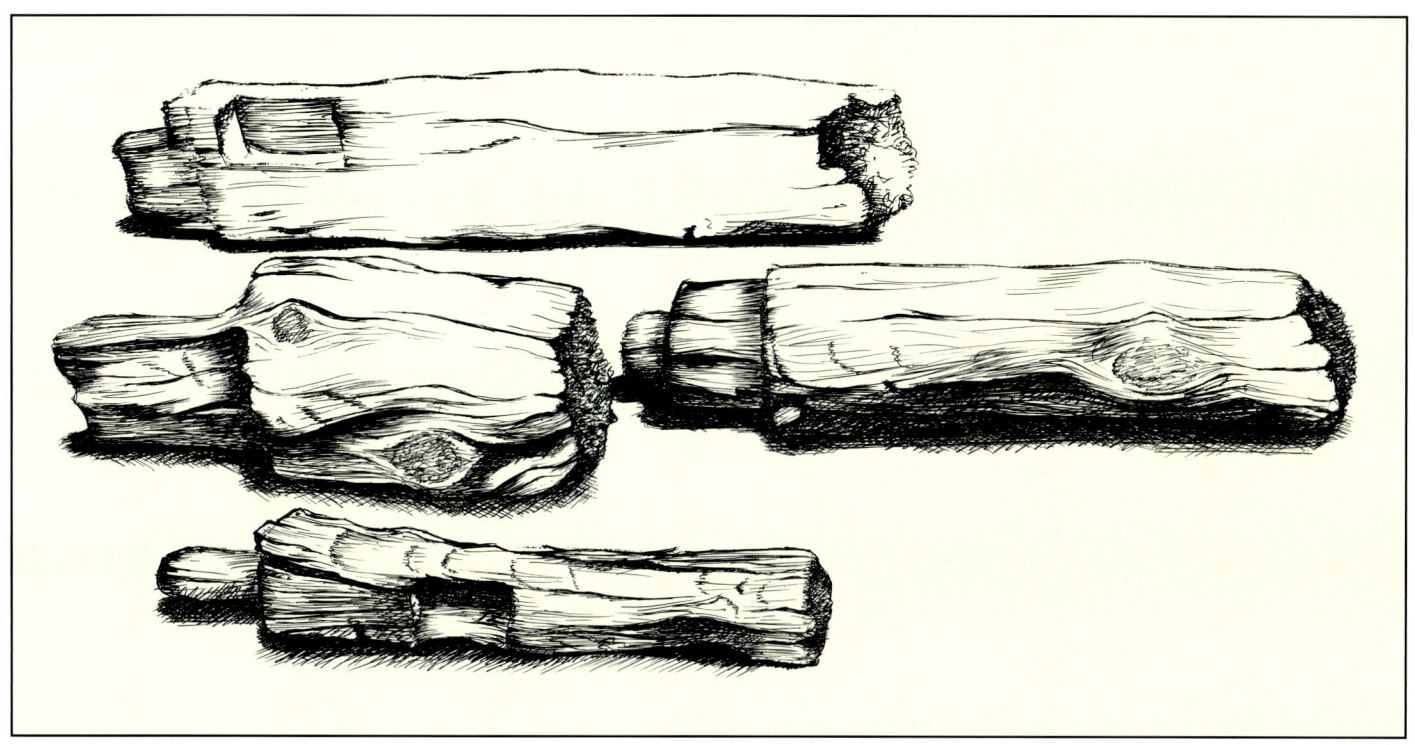

Chinese mortise and tenon joinery from 5,000 B.C.E.

Beyond the social and economic conditions hospitable to the development of timber framing, a number of environmental factors helped to ensure the longevity and continued evolution of the Chinese timber frame. China's climate is subject to significant swings in temperature and humidity, and much of the region is seismically very active. The mortise and tenon joint – and the timbers themselves – handle the expansion and contraction brought on by extremes in temperature and humidity well, and the inherent flexibility of the timber frame in an earthquake allows the structure to sway and yield, rather than remain rigid and fracture. Instead of attempting to best Mother Nature, the Chinese timbered structure was designed to yield to her. Timber frames in China have been known to withstand earthquakes of a magnitude of 7 to 8 on the Richter scale. Indeed, the worst enemies of the Chinese timber frame were not earthquakes but fire and rot. These hazards helped to motivate one of the most extraordinary innovations of any timber framing – or building – tradition in the world: modularity.

The Chinese timber structure eventually came to be rigorously codified into a series of rankings based on the intended purpose and standing of the structure within the social, political, and cultural hierarchy. Each ranking prescribed specific sizes and proportions for various components of the timber frame; thus, when a timber member of a frame required repair or replacement due to rot or other cause, the measure of that work was known by the rank of the structure in question. This system had a number of important consequences beyond ease of repair and replacement. Since the system of modularity was firmly entrenched and highly elaborated as the basis of Chinese architectural convention, no elite class of architectural practitioners ever became established there. Until the advent of modern architectural and engineering practice, building in China – as in much of the outside world – was the dominion of the craftsman. The modularity of the building method, moreover, was an expedient for the perpetuation of the system, and greatly facilitated the transfer of Chinese building technology to other cultures throughout East Asia.

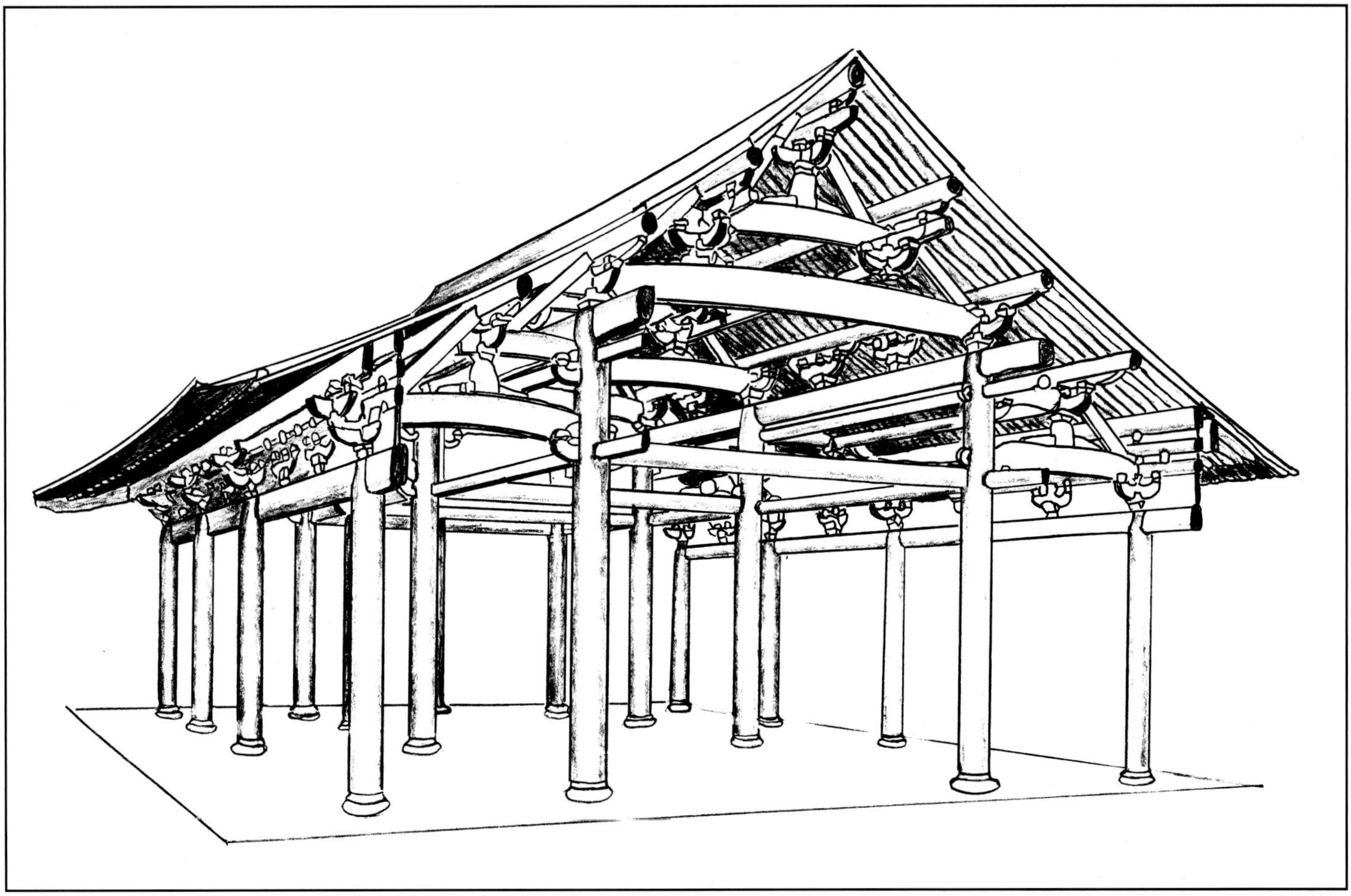

Chinese temple structure.

Evidence abounds of the wide dissemination of the highly codified Chinese system of timber construction throughout Asia, to Korea and Japan, Tibet and Northern India, and Southeast Asia. As far away as the remote recesses of the highlands of the Philippines building methods can be found that were probably influenced by early contact with Chinese traders in search of gold.

By the time contact between China and Japan began to intensify during the first millennium C.E., however, the early Japanese already had a few thousand years of timber construction behind them. Early Japanese prehistory is divided into two broad periods, the Jômon and the Yayoi. The Jômon period extends from roughly 10,500 (some scholars put it as early as 16,000) to around 750, when the Yayoi peoples, originating in the far northern regions of modern-day China, pushed across the Korean Peninsula into Japan. The Yayoi period stretched from the time of these incursions into Japan until around 200 C.E., at the time of the first wholesale importations of Chinese institutions and technology, again via the Korean Peninsula.

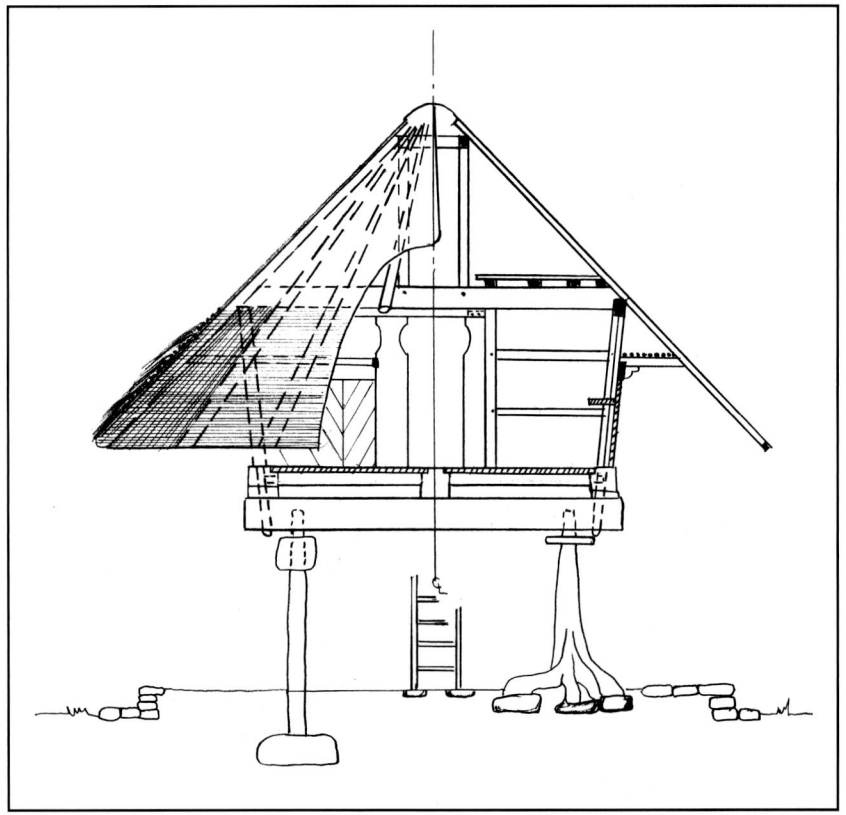

Timber-frame dwelling from the Philippine highlands.

16

The Jômon were a Mesolithic, or middle stone age, people descended from the first humans to cross the land bridges connecting the Japanese archipelago with the Korean peninsula and outer Siberia during the last Ice Age. During the Early Jômon period (c. 5,000 - 2,500 B.C.E.) settlements of sedentary agrarian tribes began to appear, and it is in these settlements that exciting evidence of early Japanese timber framing occurs. The Early Jômon dwelling was typically a circular pit hut (*tateana*, a "built-up pit"), consisting of a pit excavated about a foot or two below ground level, around which a timber framework was erected supporting a tent-like thatched roof. This form of dwelling bears a striking conceptual resemblance to the dwellings of early hominids found in Africa and Europe. In time, stilt dwellings also appeared, doubtless requiring much more sophisticated fabrication skills. For many years it was widely held that the Japanese had lagged far behind the Chinese in the development of wood building technologies in the Neolithic. Indeed, timber framing in Japan has for years been dated largely from the first sacral timber mega-structures of the Nara period (710-794 C.E.).

Archaeological finds within the last ten years, however, have done much to revise this view. While there's no doubt that Chinese timber construction strongly influenced religious building during the heyday of early imperial Japan and beyond, it now appears that there was also extensive indigenous development pre-dating the period of religious and cultural influx that came with the spread of Buddhism into Japan from China.

In 1998 timbers closely resembling those unearthed at the Hemudu site in Zhejiang, China were discovered in Toyama Prefecture on the western coast of Japan. The timber joinery, according to one report, consisted of a dadoed cross lap joint forming a tee, from what was presumed to be a stilt dwelling and was carbon-14 dated to about 2,500 B.C.E. Other reports describe the Japanese joinery found on these timbers as mortise and tenon (*watariago-shiguchi*) and add that such joinery had never before been found on artifacts from the Jômon period. Then in 2001, evidence of an even older timber structure was discovered in Oita Prefecture on the island of Kyushu, a significant distance from the earlier discovery in Toyama Prefecture. The timber in the later find consisted of what was assumed to have been a roof beam, and had a row of circular mortises carved in it to receive mating tenoned roof timbers.

Discoveries such as these have begun to influence previously held views of the extent of early contact and influence of China on Japan. Earlier views held that contact between these regions began only with the decline of the Jômon towards the middle of the first millennium B.C.E. It is now more difficult to rule out that there was an earlier transfer of technology from China to Japan.

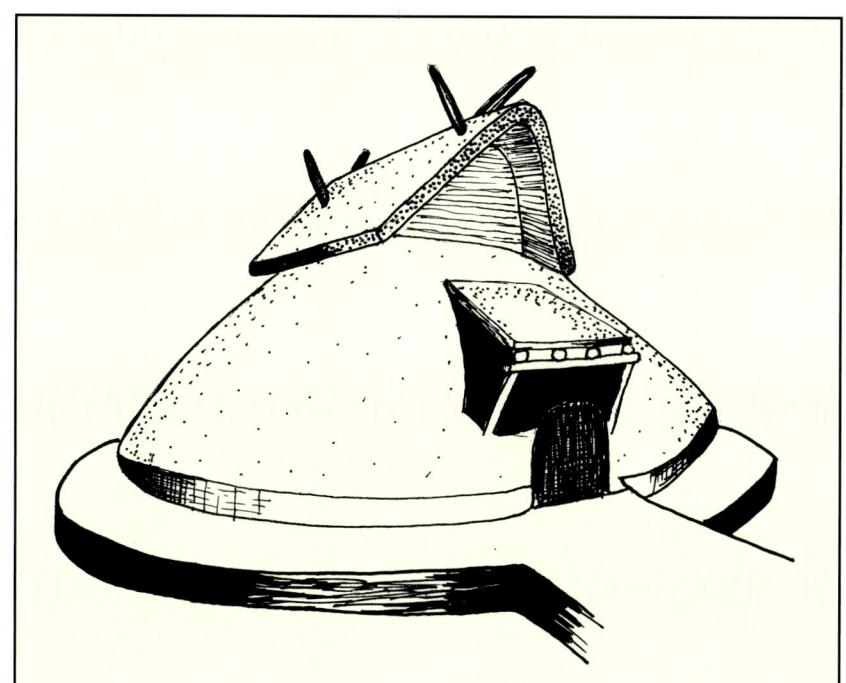

Japanese pit dwelling.

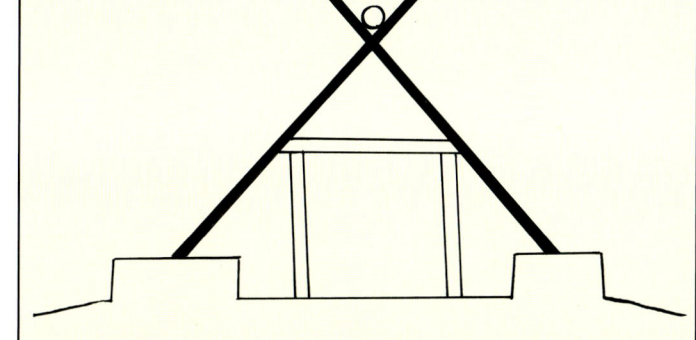

Sectional view of Japanese pit dwelling.

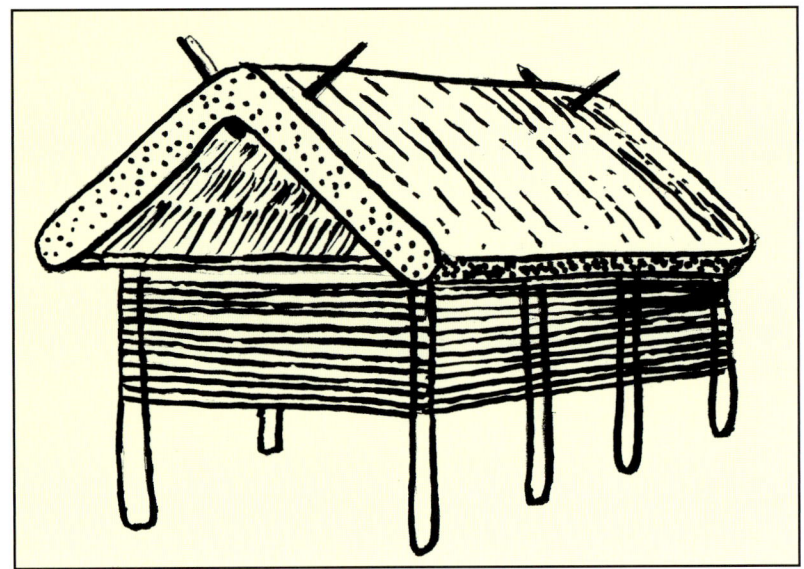

Japanese stilt dwelling.

Todai-Ji, the Hall of the Great Buddha in Nara, Japan.

A visitor to Japan easily discerns widely divergent traditions in timber construction, ranging from the simplicity of domestic architecture, or the restraint and elegance of the aristocratic dwelling, to the pomp and grandeur of Todai-Ji, the eighth century structure housing the bronze sculpture of the Great Buddha.

Even within the traditions of building for religious functions, there are dramatic differences between the sacral architecture of Buddhism, which began to reach Japan in the fifth and sixth centuries C.E., and that of Shinto, the indigenous religion that began to take shape during the Yayoi era. While the grand monuments to the Buddhist faith bear an unmistakable debt to the Chinese models of timber construction, the buildings of Shinto are stylistically closely allied with building methods of early agrarian Japan.

In the areas of joinery, too, the Buddhist architecture often favors elaborate detail, such as the "frog-leg strut" or "frog's crotch" (Japanese *kaerumata*) cantilever brackets, numerous contoured horizontal struts, and the like. Shinto shrines and much domestic architecture, on the other hand, often flaunt the elegant simplicity of their structures, giving prominent aesthetic and symbolic place to the most fundamental of structural elements. The central supporting column found in many shrines and older homes, for example, has borne great symbolic significance over the centuries as a place of abode for the deity honored at a shrine or of a protective deity for a home; indeed, on one level, the central column is regarded as the deity itself, bearing witness to the ancient animistic beliefs that supplied the foundation of Shinto.

The Japanese word for this structural element, *daikokubashira* or "pillar," has passed into the Japanese vernacular as a metaphorical reference for a person, idea or object of great importance, much as we might refer to a "pillar of society," a bulwark, or a mainstay.

Finally, it's interesting that at the center of pagoda structures – always associated with Buddhist sites – is again a *daikokubashira*, traversing the vertical distance between the granite foundation and the spire capping the structure, suggestive of the cross-fertilization between the two main religious and architectural traditions of Japan.

Japan's well-known centuries-long isolation from the outside world precluded widespread Japanese influence outside its tight cultural sphere. The same was most certainly not the case with imperial China. We have already mentioned the spread of Chinese material culture well beyond its borders in early history. The timber joinery produced during the Chinese Neolithic period is the oldest such joinery found to date anywhere in the world. This is not meant to imply, however, that the ancestry of timber construction in the West can be traced to Asian forebears. Much more, our intent here is to probe the history of timber construction in its infancy in order to tease out of this narrative some insight into the primal attraction of the human spirit to this method of building. Timber framing in the West may well have evolved in utter isolation from the early achievements of the Chinese, yet the forebears of Western timber construction found in crude early shelters and their path towards refinement paralleled in large part those of the Chinese.

Japanese domestic architecture.

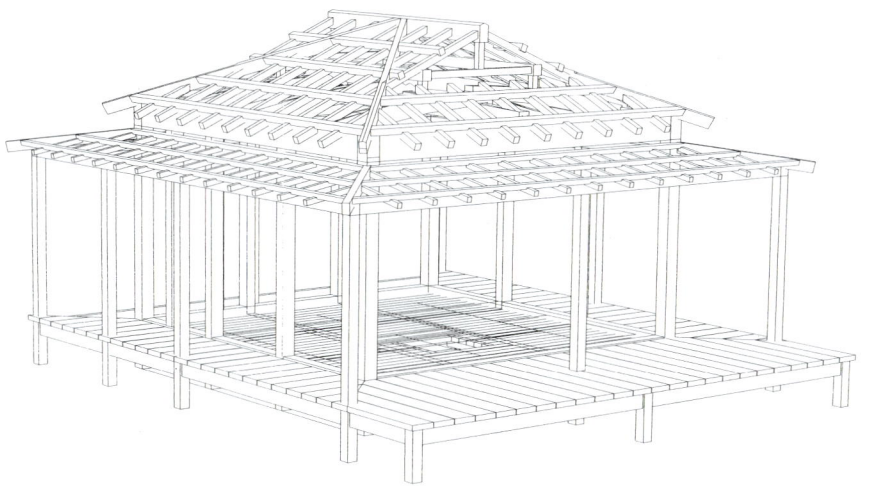

Japanese aristocrat's pavilion.

The Great Buddha, with "frog's crotch" brackets in foreground.

Timber Construction in the West – The Mediterranean

We have seen that timber construction existed in early dynastic Egypt, although its architectural use did not extend beyond lintel-like roof timbers until much later. Records exist of the importation of cedar timbers from Lebanon, and of the Egyptian demand for the increasingly scarce commodity, pushing the reach of their commerce further around the Eastern Mediterranean basin, into Asia Minor, the Caucasus, and beyond.

Within the cultural and economic orbit of Egyptian civilization in the early to middle bronze age (3,500 to 1,600 B.C.E.) another civilization emerged that in time rivaled the cultural and economic achievements of the Egyptians – the Minoans. The home of this civilization, the island of Crete, had been the site of Neolithic settlements as early as 7,000 B.C.E., although no known remains of timber construction from this early period exist. Judging from timber use in remaining portions of the large palace complex at Knossos, dating from approximately 1,700 to 1,300 B.C.E., however, timber construction was already well developed in the heyday of Minoan civilization.

Similar construction methods, hybrids of stone and timber construction, predominated in the large-scale building of the Hittite civilization of Asia Minor (modern-day North-Central Turkey), and the Mycenaean civilization – the predecessor of Hellenistic civilization – in roughly the same period. The Minoans flourished for a relatively brief period. Their decline has been linked to the decimation of their forests and aridization of their island, which sounded the death knell for their primary industry of bronze smelting. In much the same manner, the lush cedar forests of the Lebanon were felled into oblivion by untold generations of Phoenicians, their predecessors and successors. Before the depletion of the forests of the Eastern Mediterranean region had run its full course, however, the torch of civilization had been carried to another great culture and major contributor to the history of architecture in the West, Greece.

Greek architecture is widely identified by the iconic image of a temple ruin – a bleached white behemoth set in a bucolic mountain fastness, often with more of its structure strewn in fragments about the ground than standing. Ironically, these great stone monuments are perhaps the best remaining repositories of knowledge about the earlier Greek building methods, which relied largely on massive timber members. Before the forests of the Eastern Mediterranean region had been exhausted, ancient Greece had abundant supplies of oak, and many accounts describe early sacral architecture constructed entirely of timber. Vase paintings of the oldest Doric order of architecture depict components that appear to be wooden, and Vitruvius, the first century B.C.E. Roman architect and architectural historian, wrote that the forms of classical Greek architecture derived from the features of earlier wooden buildings.

Reconstruction of the Palace of Knossos on the island of Crete, showing the misguided use of concrete to simulate what was once a heavy timber frame in-filled with rubble.

Early Greek timbered antecedents of temple architecture.

The Temple of Hera/Megaron.

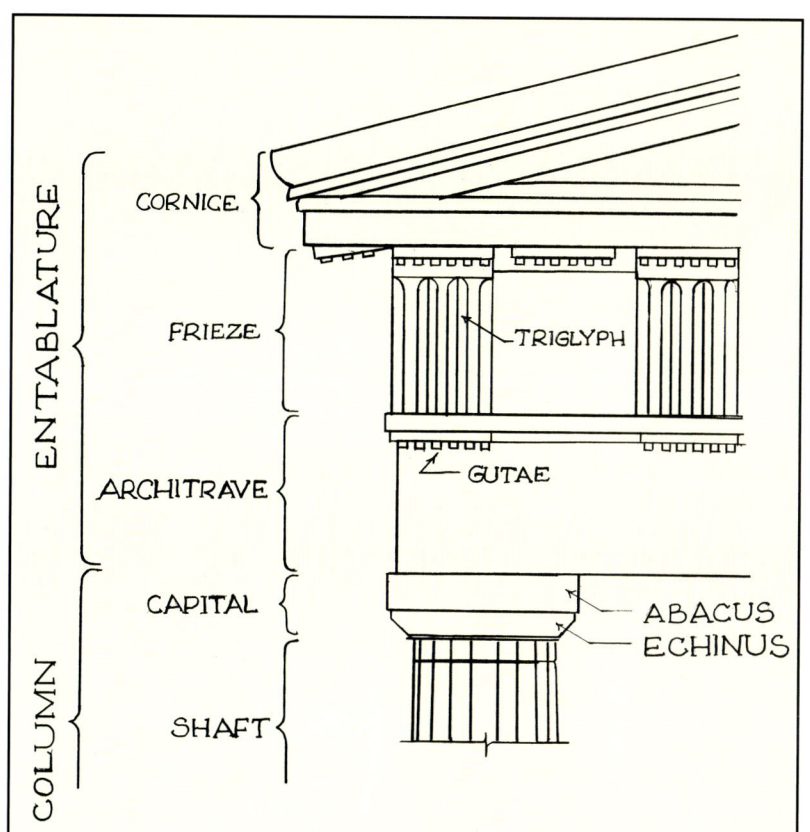

Entablature of the Greek orders.

Lycian stone tomb mimicking timber construction.

Portal of a timber-inspired tomb carved into a cliff in Lycia, Asia Minor (present day South-West Turkey)

According to accounts from Vitruvius, as the Greeks' transition to building in marble and limestone progressed, functional elements of the earlier timber building method were translated into stone. Perhaps most conspicuously, the entablature – the portion of the Greek temple edifice resting on the columns – contained a great many details descended from wooden ancestors. The triglyphs, for example, the triple-grooved vertical stone slab projecting from the frieze, are thought to represent the slabs of wood affixed to the jutting roof timbers to protect them from rain and rot; the six guttae immediately below the triglyph may well have been wooden pegs inserted to hold the beam in place. Even the fluting of the Doric order columns suggest a reference to the hewing used to round the heavy tree trunks thought to have been the first columns. Large-scale sacral architecture in wood continued to be built well into the archaic period in ancient Greece (800-600 B.C.E.), and some accounts describe ongoing gradual replacement of individual timber components with marble elements until much later in history.

Our knowledge of early Greek timber construction relies chiefly on conjecture due to the lack of detailed and reliable accounts, and because no examples have survived. Of those massive timber structures known to have existed, it is hard to imagine their construction without joinery, and certainly representations of timber construction in marble make allusion to such joinery techniques. For the most part, however, the later Greek use of timber was restricted to roof and ceiling structures. This is not surprising, considering the growing scarcity of timber resources at the time and the underlying structural paradigm that prevailed in the design of large-scale architecture throughout the Mediterranean region up until Roman times. The structures produced in this period are referred to as "trabeated" and are based on the fundamental unit of two vertical posts supporting a horizontal lintel. (The term *trabeated* derives from the Latin for beam – *trab* or *trabes* – and, interestingly, is related to a host of words in Indo-European languages referring to dwellings, building, and villages.) Unlike its classical counterpart, the "arcuated" system, the trabeated system does not produce diagonal or outward thrust, and so it may seem that there was little impetus for the Greeks to develop sophisticated methods of timber joinery and construction.

The trabeated structural system and reliance on profuse internal intercolumniation of Greek structures notwithstanding, however, recent scholarship has proposed the existence of a highly developed timber framing technology that both complemented and rivaled the exquisiteness of the stone masonry of Greek architecture. George Izenour, in his book *Roofed Theaters of Classical Antiquity* (1992), has provocatively argued that many of the Greek and Roman theaters heretofore thought of as open air affairs were in fact often fully enclosed and roofed. The clear, unsupported spans that would have been required to erect a roof over these structures would severely challenge even the technical prowess of many contemporary timber framers, ranging, as they did in classical Greece, to more than 70 feet. Their execution without the aid of highly sophisticated timber truss technology is quite improbable.

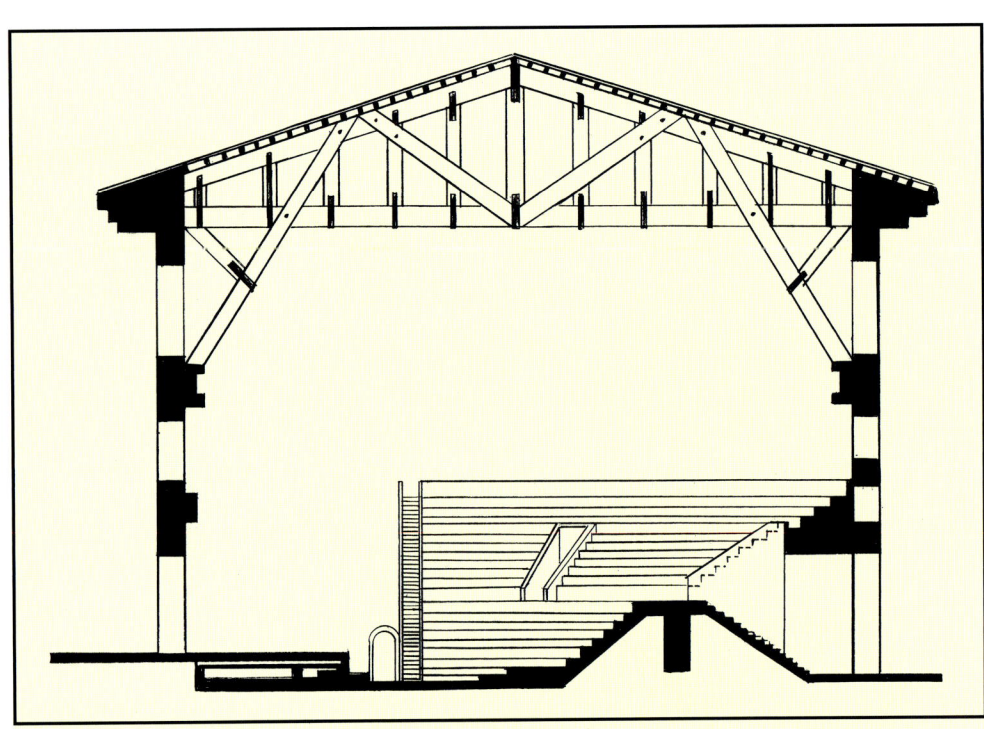

Roofed amphitheater of classical antiquity.

The applications of timber framing in Greece were, of course, never limited to the opulence and grandeur of sacral and public architecture. We are safe in assuming that Greek domestic architecture continued to use timbers as a component of hybridized construction methods, such as the "half-timbered" structures of stone, rubble, and heavy timber illustrated in the discussion of Minoan architectural relics above. Evidence of this method of timber construction has been found in Greek-influenced cities and towns throughout the Mediterranean. The Greek use of heavy roof and ceiling timbers, and the composite "half-timbered" structures fully conform to our definition of a hybrid structure – the combination of differing materials and building methods to handle different components of the loads imposed on a structure.

Moreover, timber technology in Greece found employment in areas other than architecture. History is full of the curious and bizarre, such as the well-preserved records of a 40-foot tall timber-framed siege engine built for the Battle of Moyta, waged by the Greeks of Syracuse against the Carthaginians in 349 B.C.E.

What these examples are meant to illustrate is the changing nature of timber use in the Greek building arts. The Greek builder grasped the underlying principles of the structural challenges they faced in the abstract, and so began to allocate and manipulate materials in a manner that made optimal use of material properties. The massive, hulking forms of the Doric order are still firmly rooted in the heavy timber megaron of its Mycenaean ancestry (see the drawing of the early Greek Temple of Hera above) with trunk-like columns supporting enormous stone lintels. In these structures the stone has not yet fully transcended its megalithic nature, just as its timbered antecedents had not escaped their tree-like identities. With the advent of the truss structures of the roofed amphitheater and the siege engine, the forces that challenged the Greek builder were understood in the abstract; timber no longer owed its shape to the tree from which it was hewn, but to the *function* it must perform.

As the evolution of the Greek architectural orders progressed, this memorialization of an earlier method of building took on ever more stylized forms; the *echinus* and *abacus* (see illustration of architrave details above) of the Doric order, even the Ionic volute capitals, are conceptually behind the almost baroque stylization of the Corinthian acanthus leaf capital. Perhaps it was the growing scarcity of the original materials of construction that motivated the nostalgia inherent in these memorializing gestures; perhaps it was a romantic sense of lost innocence that accompanied the growing abstraction of the building arts. The Greek builders were not the first to take inspiration for the forms of their architectural embellishment from earlier building methods. The Egyptians had their papyrus bundle-inspired columns, and the acanthus leaves of the Corinthian order of Greek architecture had clear Egyptian antecedents. But it is in the architectural practice of ancient Greece that the commingled processes of abstraction and memorialization fertilized the seed of the rationality that came to dominate the architecture of Greece's successor in the Mediterranean, Rome.

Rome: Utilitas – Firmitas – Venustas

In the waning days of the Hellenistic hegemony over the Eastern Mediterranean Greek civilization suffered countless humiliations at the hands of the Romans. Yet if imitation is indeed the sincerest form of flattery, it suffered those humiliations from atop a lofty pedestal. Much has been written of Rome's cultural debt to Ancient Greece, from the formation of Rome's political and social institutions to the outward forms of her architecture, from the Roman penchant for the sculptural arts of Greece, to education, philosophy, and science. Nevertheless, while this debt is indisputable, it scants Rome's important – and numerous – contributions to the building arts of the West. Yet, among its many contributions, ancient Rome is generally credited with the invention of concrete – certainly a momentous development in the building arts – as well as the development and possibly the invention of the arch. (Often attributed to Etruscan civilization, cf. Jean-Pierre Adam, *Roman Building, Materials and Techniques*, 1994; *p.158*) As such, Roman architecture helped to initiate the transition from the trabeated structure of the Egyptians and Greeks to the arcuated structures that dominated the architectural imagination of the West through the medieval period down to the neo-Classical movements of the sixteenth to twentieth centuries.

The Roman builder's fascination with the arch overshadows the role of timber construction in the historical narrative. The remains of the Coliseum, the Forum Romanum, the Pantheon – all are eloquent testament to the engineering prowess of the Romans. Timber in architecture appears to have played a secondary role in the *aesthetics* of architectural expression. Indeed, while the trajectory of timber construction arcs steadily upward through history, timber framing in the West was not to break this mold until much later. The utilitarian ethos of timber construction persisted well into modern times, the skeletal timbered structure often being relegated to the concealed recesses of a structure – somewhat akin to the cavities in stud-walled structures of present-day America – hidden away for none but the builder to see, and serving often merely as support for the ornamental elements of a building. As we will see, this persistent theme bears directly on our present-day fascination with the timber frame, since its direct ancestor – the heavy timbered dwellings of the eighteenth and nineteenth centuries in America had still not broken free of the constraints of a strictly utilitarian frame of reference. The timber frame revival of the early seventies in America, indeed, owes much to an ideology of the essential in the building arts – to the urge to strip away the superfluous, the deceptive, and the deracinated elements of our mass-produced housing developments.

Despite the relative sparseness of the historical record on Roman timber framing, we've been left with tantalizing vestiges of the ingenuity of the Roman builder's use of timber. In domestic architecture, the Roman builder shared in the time-honored legacy of Mediterranean timber construction as an adjunct to stone, much as in the examples we have seen of Minoa and Asia Minor. One of the richest repositories of the evidence for the use of "half-timbered" construction is in the haunting sites of Pompeii and Herculaneum, buried for centuries under layers of compacted volcanic ash. Here the charred timbers of what was called *opus craticium* have been found still embedded in their masses of rubble or unbaked clay, some still with the vestigial plaster rendering that kept the timber structure out of view. These structures are the forebears of the half-timbered structures of Northern Europe. In the vernacular building arts of Rome, even the technique of wattle and daub was use to enclosed timbered structures, much as their North European successors.

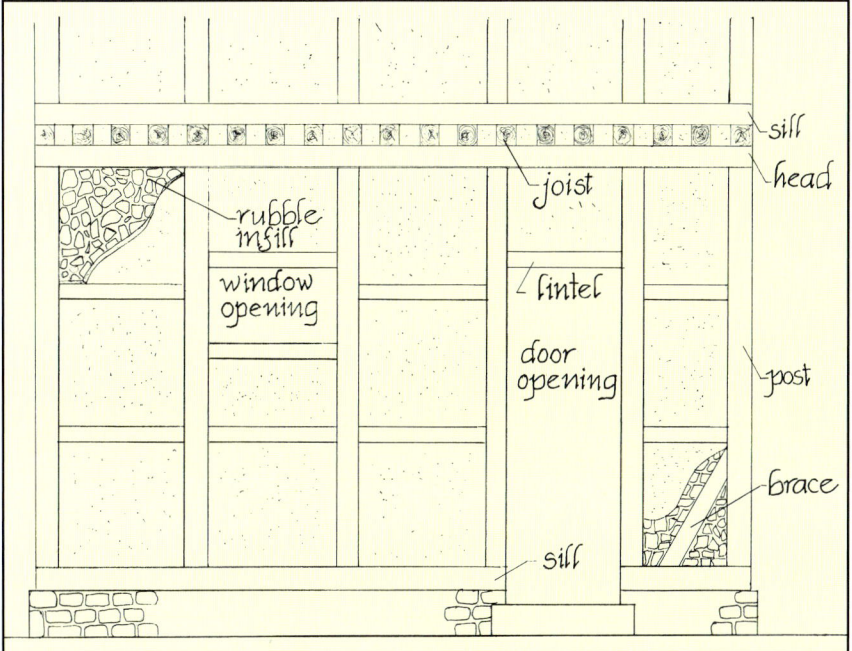

Roman *opus craticium*, or half-timbering.

Roman wattle and daub, infill for half-timbered structures.

Of a more conjectural nature is the record of the Roman's use of elaborate systems of trusswork to support masonry arches and vaults during the process of construction before they became self-supporting. No reliable written or pictorial record is known to exist of these structures – which are called the "centring" for concrete and masonry works – but speculative extrapolation from later medieval pictorial records demonstrates early mastery of the engineering principles of the truss. A truly fundamental development in the history of building, the truss structure relies on the triangulation of members that transfer loads downward to the earth. It may be wrong to ascribe the invention of the truss to the Romans; it is nonetheless true that the Romans stood at the fountainhead of European timber framing, marching, as did their armies, over vast reaches of the European continent with their technologies and culture in tow.

One particularly fascinating indication of the Roman's timber framing prowess is a depiction of the bridge built by Roman legionnaires over the Danube River in the year 104 C.E. The unusual configuration of the timbers supporting the superstructure appears to be unique in the history of timbered bridges. The timber substructure consists of units performing structural work much in the manner of the wedge-shaped stone of the Roman arch, rather than the more common triangulation of timber members.

The Romans knew well the structural potential of the triangulated truss, using it in the roof structures of the concrete and marble-veneered monuments, to the grandeur of their civilization. These truss structures existed alongside the more rudimentary post and lintel configurations, often combined with stone elements. In the end, the limitation of timber framing in Roman building arts was a function of the relative scarcity of wood as a building material; of the abundance of stone; and of the desire of neophytic Roman culture to emulate the imposing grandeur of Hellenistic Greece. It does not appear that a lack of technical and engineering expertise influenced in any way the relative scarcity of Roman timber framing.

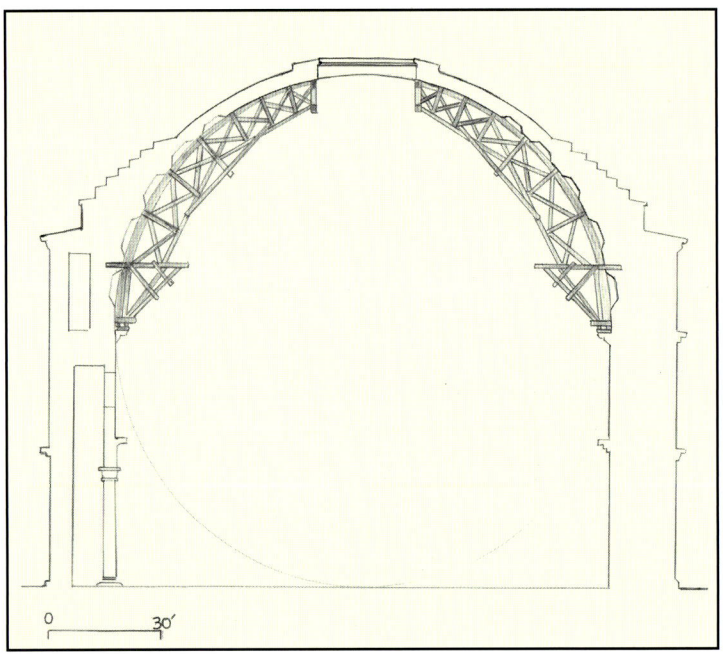

Roman "centring."

Trajan's bridge over the Danube.

Timber arrangement of Trajan's bridge over the Danube.

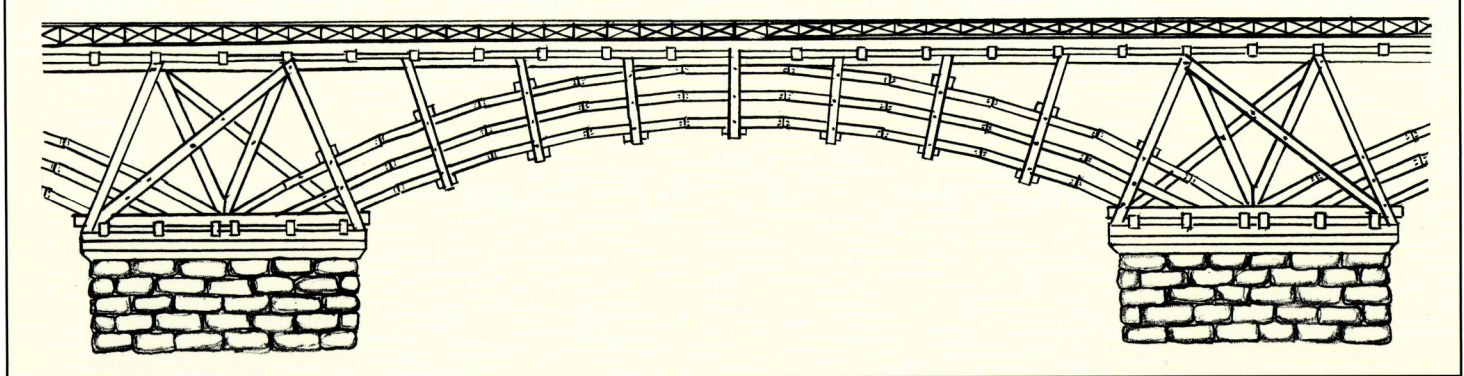

Northern Europe in the Medieval and Renaissance Periods

By the time Roman dominance over Northern Europe had begun its decline, timber framing, like most other Roman technologies, had been widely spread throughout the region. There is scant evidence of sophisticated timber framing, on a par with that of the Romans or the Greeks, in Northern Europe before the tenth or eleventh centuries. Earlier examples of wood construction, particularly in Anglo-Saxon England, were more reminiscent of log construction, and were relatively modest in scale, while continuing to demonstrate inventiveness and skill in the manipulation of the materials. Timber castles using the wattle and daub or rubble infill carried on the traditions stretching back through Rome to pre-Hellenic civilizations of Asia Minor. Prior to the high medieval period (from the eleventh to the end of the thirteenth centuries) timber continued to be used in a manner similar to that seen in the Mediterranean civilizations in a kind of stone & timber hybrid. It's likely that adverse socio-economic conditions played the decisive role in this period of relative stagnation. Society in the early Middle Ages simply did not produce the prosperity necessary to fund building on the scale that would stimulate the development of the engineering science of timber construction. As Northern Europe emerged from the so-called Dark Ages and the societies of the High Medieval period began to flourish, timber construction experienced a flowering unlike anything previously seen in the West.

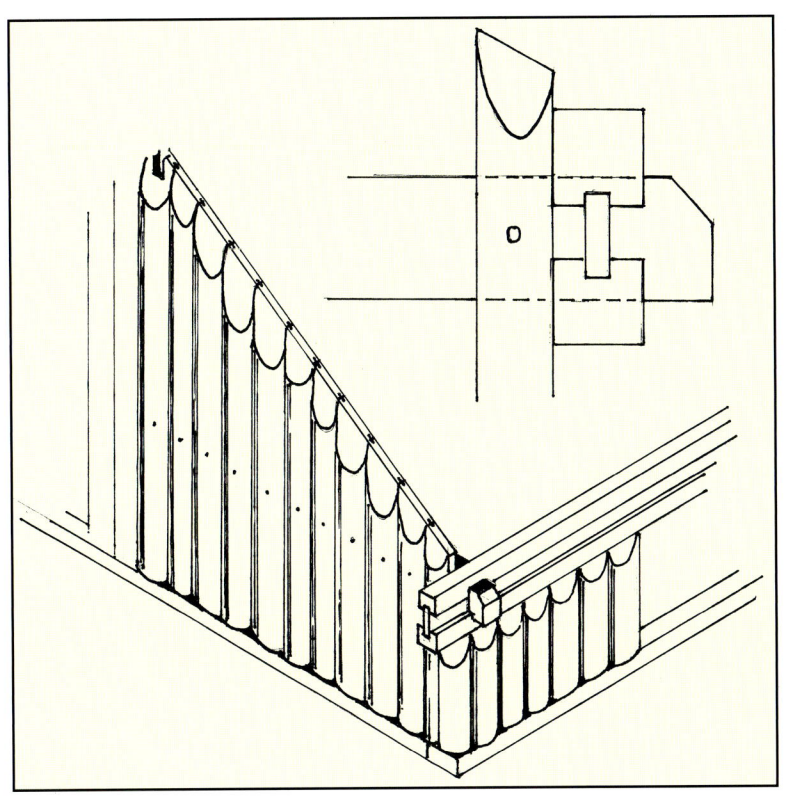

Early Anglo-Saxon log and timber construction.

Early Anglo-Saxon timber castle.

By the middle of the eleventh century C.E., timber construction was widely used in ambitious and daring structures, quite frequently large churches and cathedrals with massive stone walls and buttresses and soaring, steeply-pitched roof systems, where the art and science of the timber framer were at times on full display. More often, however, these heavily timbered structures were concealed above masonry vaulting or suspended wooden ceilings, and the rough and unfinished appearance of some timber structures leads one to believe that timbers were only ever left exposed due more to a lack of sufficient resources than to an aesthetic appreciation of the timbered structure. On the continent, in Northern France and elsewhere, the norm was the masonry vault, above which the roof superstructure stood. The high medieval period in Britain saw the development of an exception to this rule in the construction of elaborately embellished wooden structures with refined curvatures, polished finishes, an exuberant use of timber resources, ornate traceries, and intricately molded columns and structural members.

Medieval French domestic building, showing timber structure confined to roof structure.

Cathedral with masonry vault and concealed timber roof structure.

These large, generations-long ecclesiastical works were more the exception in timber use in the building arts. Timbers were massive and numerous, required by the structural challenges imposed upon them. Apart from barn structures that served tax authorities and large landholders, the historical record of timber framing for domestic use is incomplete. In Britain, cruck frames were common in barn structures, leading one to believe that domestic structures may well have made use of smaller, less perfectly formed timbers that would have been unacceptable for cathedral construction.

The rise of urban living during the northern Renaissance, however, brought another quantum leap forward in the method and science of timber construction. As work on gargantuan religious projects decelerated, builders turned their attention to constructing the cities that would accommodate burgeoning mercantile activities and an expanding middle class. At its most conspicuous, the art of timber construction migrated to the province of domestic building, responding to the desire of the middle classes for flamboyant exhibition of their newfound prosperity. In the process, the construction method we have observed reaching back at least to Minoan civilization – walls consisting of timbered frameworks in-filled with rubble, stone, masonry or wattle and daub – was revived to stunning visual effect.

The term "half-timbered" is believed to have entered the popular lexicon in 1823 with the publication of Mary Martha Sherwood's novel *The Lady of the Manor*. The term refers to timber frame structures whose members are in-filled with wattle and daub or brick. The term can be misleading since the members were, in fact, full timbers. Sherwood was primarily a writer of children's literature, so it is likely she coined the term in an attempt to illustrate that in such buildings half (or one side) of the timber is visible on the interior and the other half is visible on the exterior. Another popular term for such dwellings is "black and whites," a term which is perhaps more accurate and descriptive.

The half-timbered towns and cities of Northern Europe romanticized in Sherwood's novels present a feast for the eyes, with serried ranks of houses lining the narrow cobble-stoned streets, extravagantly framed with a myriad of braces, corbelled jetties, and decorative quatrefoils, each house vying for ascendancy over its neighbor. Half-timbered houses and civic structures provide an enduring visual record of the exploding population of the High Renaissance, and of the thriving craft of the timber framer.

Along with this expanding population came a much altered economics of building. Even while the prosperity of the growing middle classes allowed greater expenditures on dwellings and shop premises, the growing scarcity of large stands of timber led to new techniques of timber construction, using numerous small timbers, where once massive timbers might have been used. By the end of the High Renaissance in Northern Europe, the resources necessary for the lavish use of timber had dwindled, and new building methods relying more heavily on the techniques of masonry construction came to dominate. Timber framing – still indispensable for the construction of roofs, floors, and other structural elements – once again began to vanish behind the veneer of ornament and decoration that the middle and upper classes now enlisted in their pursuit of status and gentility.

Half-timbered houses in Braubach, Germany.

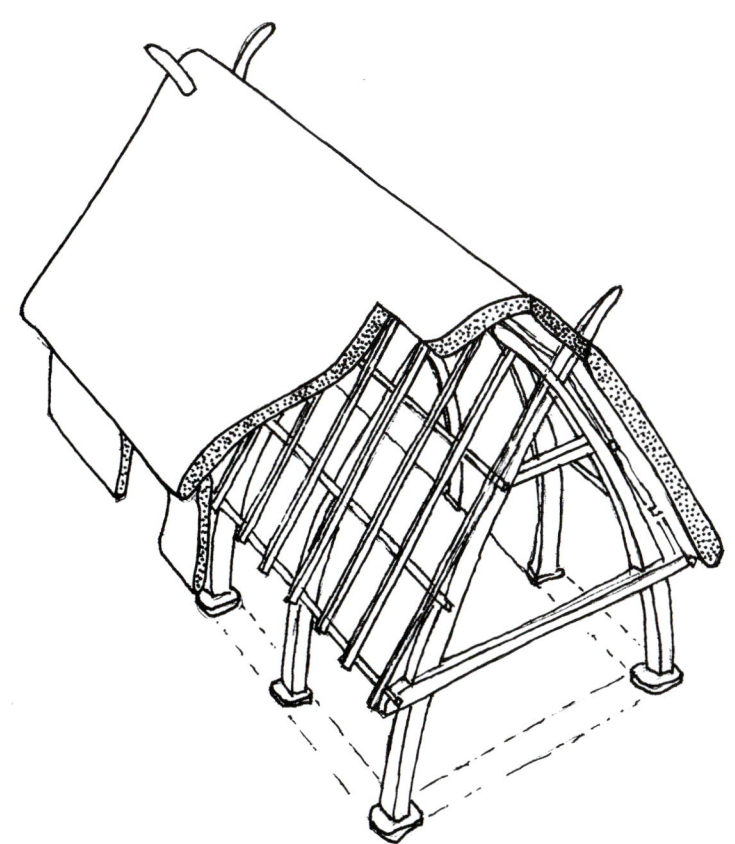

English cruck frame.

Half-timber houses in Hornburg, Germany.

Extravagant half-timbering at Little Moreton Hall, Cheshire, England.

Timber Construction on American Soil

This was the historical context out of which timber framing in colonial America emerged. Yet while the return of timber construction to the sphere of utility was already established by the time of the earliest colonization of the Americas, this was not the primary factor influencing the unique development of timber framing in America. The first settlers may well have gaped in amazement at the vast expanses of virgin wilderness that lay before them. The timber framers among them surely appreciated the unfettered freedom of design and fabrication that this seemingly inexhaustible resource offered them. Drawing largely on the British traditions of joinery and frame design, but free of the limitations imposed by the scarcity of large timbers, the early American timber wrights fashioned unadorned, utilitarian frames that exploited timbers of great length and girth.

Timber framing in America enjoyed ascendancy over other building methods for much of America's early history. The Plymouth settlement, one of the earliest beachheads of the multitudes of immigrants to come to the New World, was itself the site of the first rude timber frames erected on American soil. All along the Eastern seaboard and inland for a hundred or so miles, from New England down to the Florida Keys and into the Caribbean, timber framing was the predominant form of construction in America up to the mid-1800s. Where stone was readily available timbers formed the interior skeleton and roof for stone walls; in the seaport towns and cities timbers were integrated in much the same manner with bricks, a resource readily available because of its use as ship ballast; riven clapboard attached directly to timbers was another common method of enclosure; in inland homesteads, log

The Kifer House, Strasburg, Pennsylvania.

homes provided a toe-hold for early settlers, only to be replaced with timber framed structures as soon as possible. And as soon as the prosperity of these early timber-framed settlements allowed, timbers were once again hidden away behind plaster and lath to please more refined tastes.

The surging waves of immigration that began in the early to middle 1800s created population pressures in the booming urban centers of the east, resulting in an ever-growing trend towards settlement of the American interior. The explosive population growth of this period – and the consequent dispersion of immigrants across the continent – created a growing demand for a method of construction that was cheaper and faster, and that required a lower level of skill from its practitioners. Local sawmills sprouted up across the nation to produce light studs, and mass-produced cut steel nails made assembly faster and easier. The American network of rail transport, once the envy of the Western hemisphere, sped the materials of home construction to every corner of the land.

Date carving on lintel of Kifer house door.

The Golden Plough Tavern circa 1741 is the oldest building in York, Pennsylvania, once the capital of the United States. This tavern is a hybrid, with the lower level of log construction and the upper level timber framed. It was here that the Marquis de Lafayette helped defuse a movement by Generals Horatio Gates, Thomas Conway, and others to remove General George Washington from his position. In toasting General Washington, Lafayette, who delegated himself spokesman for the French court, conveyed the position that France equated Washington with the American cause and could not conceive of another leader. The movement lost momentum before it could reach the weight of a plot.

The new construction method debuted in Chicago in 1833, and came, for a time, to be called "Chicago Framing." By the 1870s, Chicago framing had established itself throughout the United States. Enough of a fond collective memory of the timber wright's craft remained, however, to earn Chicago framing the derisive moniker "balloon framing," due to its lightness and perceived insubstantiality. By the beginning decades of the twentieth century, balloon framing gave way to a simpler and sounder method first called "Western framing," then later "platform framing." Platform framing is the method of construction in common use today. It differs from balloon framing in its method of providing support for upper floors. In balloon framing, an upper floor is attached to stud-framed walls, essentially hanging from them. In platform framing, a single-story wall supports the floor above, with upper story walls resting on the upper floor framing.

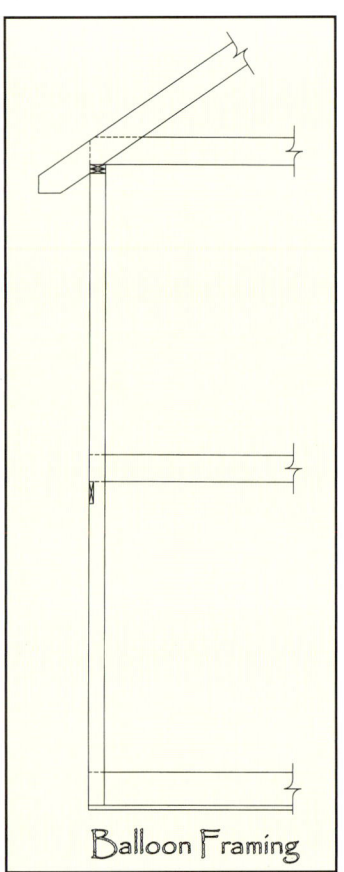 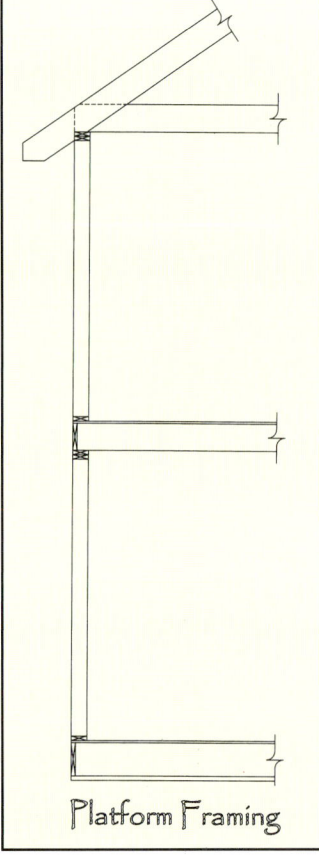

In the face of the challenges to its dominance over other building methods in America, timber framing entered a period of decline towards the end of the nineteenth century. Utilitarian structures – warehouses and factory buildings, and barns in particular – continued to employ the methods of timber framing for a time, and have been continuously erected to this day by the Anabaptists of Pennsylvania, Ohio, Indiana, and elsewhere. Heavy timbers found new application in the construction of railroad bridges and trestles as well as in providing the floor systems for early twentieth century industrial buildings. Some of these now 100-year-old buildings are being gradually "mined" for their massive timbers. The transportation and industrial applications for heavy timbers, however, veered away from traditional timber framing in their use of iron and steel connecting hardware. Ultimately, steel replaced the timbers entirely in such applications. With these transitions, timber framing entered a seventy-year period of suspended animation, during which the craft had few practitioners other than the Amish.

Bethany United Methodist Church, Red Lion, Pennsylvania. This church has both a timber frame roof structure on display, and one hidden away above the ceiling.

A turn of the century factory building in Columbia, Pennsylvania. This is the last remaining section of what was once a large factory complex with massive floor and roof timbers. The other sections have been "mined" for their timbers for the last twenty years.

Habitat for Humanity/Timber Framers Guild timber raising in 1989, Hanover, Pennsylvania.

The American Revival

It was the baby boomer generation that brought about the renaissance of timber framing, beginning in the early nineteen seventies. The pursuit of the essential and uncomplicated values of bygone times, the rejection of the values of a mass consumption society, together with a romantic sense of lost innocence motivated the revival of the crafts and trades that were thought to embody a greater sense of authenticity.

One of these trades was the art and science of timber framing. The resurgence of this lost craft has been gathering momentum ever since. In 1977 the first American book on timber framing, *The Timber Frame House* by Stewart Elliot, was published, only to be amplified and supplemented a few years later by Tedd Benson's *The Timber House, Revival of a Forgotten Craft*. The latter achieved something of a cult following among the first and second wave of revivalists. By 1984, the ranks of American timber framers had swelled to the point that organization seemed desirable, and the formation of the Timber Framers Guild of North America was the result. The organization of the first annual conference in Hancock, Massachusetts, followed the next year and drew close to 200 enthusiasts.

Two other events were helpful in propelling the timber framing revival into national consciousness. The first of these occurred in 1989, when the Timber Framers Guild of North America coordinated a project with the York, Pennsylvania, chapter of Habitat for Humanity. Timber framers from across America and from several foreign countries converged on Hanover, Pennsylvania, donating material and skill to two needy families and erected two timber frames and enclosed them in structural insulating panels. Habitat for Humanity volunteers prepared the sites and finished out the two homes, and WHYY from Philadelphia and the British Broadcasting Corporation covered the event in television broadcasts. Two years later "This Old House" with Norm Abrams featured a timber frame project in Concord, Massachusetts; the show has been re-broadcast ever since.

The Timber Framers Guild of North America eventually dropped the phrase "of North America" due to the growing influx of members from abroad. At least twenty nations are now represented on the Timber Framers Guild membership roles, now grown to over 1,800 individual and group members. The TFG has since spawned three additional organizations: the Traditional Timber Frame Research and Advisory Group, focusing on the documentation, repair, preservation, reconstruction and reproduction of historic timber frame structures; the Timber Frame Business Council, an affiliate organization made up of company memberships and dedicated to strengthening the timber frame industry; and the Timber Frame Engineering Council, dedicated to advancing the science of timber frame design.

In the first two decades of the revival, the vast majority of timber-framed structures were residential. As awareness of the possibilities expanded, timber framing began to appear in commercial and institutional structures, such as museums, wineries, churches, restaurants, country club and golf course clubhouses, and libraries. Since timber framing is a method of construction rather than a style, it remains an eminently effective and flexible complement to virtually any architectural project. It has been employed in building projects ranging from period reproductions to sleek and minimalist architectural statements. The appeal of timber framing today lies in its ability to fold architectural, structural, and sculptural character into a single expressive whole. People will always feel attracted to and comforted by its visual, tactile, and emotional qualities. While the growth of timber framing has been strong and constant, it will never again become the main construction method of America. Yet it has re-entered the sphere of the building arts as a strong and viable alternative to conventional building methods, or, even more broadly, as a method that can be artfully integrated into conventionally built structures.

Interestingly, the first years of the timber framing revival saw the production of timber frames influenced largely by the building methods of early American timber wrights. Many of the timber frames from the 1970s were typical New England saltbox style homes, in most cases being what is now referred to as whole-house timber frames. A whole-house timber frame is one in which every exterior wall and many interior rooms and spaces are defined and supported by timber elements. Even sub-floors separating the basement from the first floor were often framed with heavy timbers.

Yet the America of the late twentieth and early twenty-first centuries is not the America of the 1600 or 1700s. Early American timber framers drew raw materials for their craft from what seemed a virtually inexhaustible supply of timber. Consequently, early American timber frames at times made extravagant use of this resource, as much for the abundance of timber as for its ease of fabrication and effectiveness as a building material. Enormous old growth timbers were commonly used to solve structural challenges. The resulting design and appearance of American timber framing often differed considerably from its European precursors.

The American revival of timber framing followed the lead of these early craftsmen. Had we looked back across the ocean to our timber-framing forebears, had we studied the history of the craft more attentively, indeed, had we studied the surviving European craft of timber framing, we would have drawn different lessons to guide the early revival. We would have realized that hybrids – the combination of heavy timber with other materials and building methods – are as much a part of the history of timber framing as are the mortise and tenon and the truss. As our historical survey has attempted to demonstrate, *the hybrid was the first and most enduring form of timber framing.*

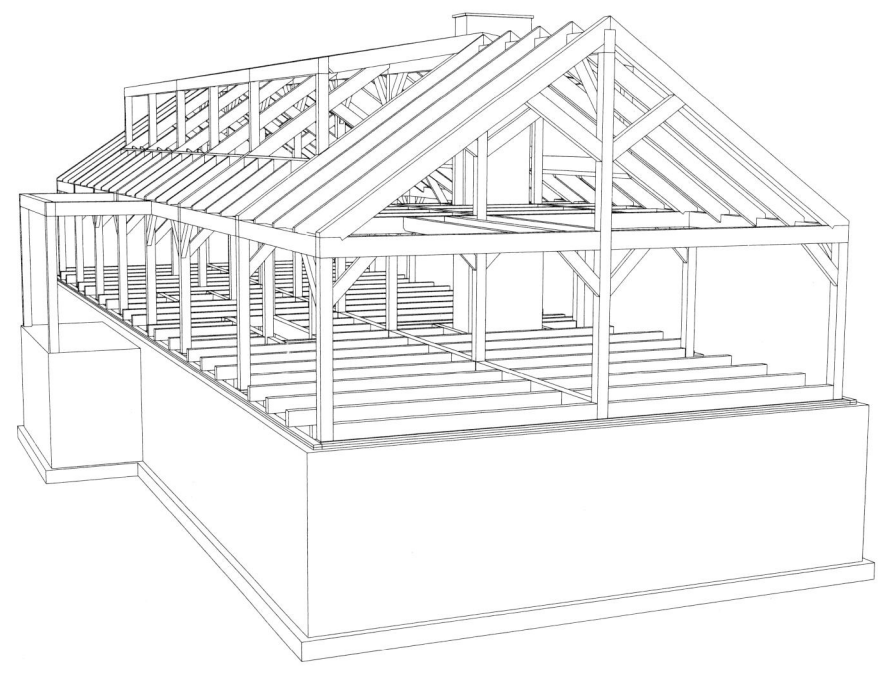

A contemporary whole house timber frame.

THE CASE FOR HYBRID TIMBER FRAMES

As we have seen, the search for the elemental values of living and dwelling, and the rejection of the perceived perversion of those values by modern mass society, helped to drive the early timber frame revival. A sense among the younger generation of a general decline in moral, cultural, social, and even technological standards – a sense of alienation from tradition – characterized the social upheaval of the sixties.

In this roiling social context the timber frames of early America signified an authenticity – now lost – in the realm of dwelling in harmony with the natural condition of humankind. The revival of the craft of the timberwright assumed symbolic dimensions in the pursuit of social and cultural renewal. Accordingly it's hardly surprising that out of the passion of the first timber frame revivalists, and out of the sheer ambition of their early program – the rejuvenation of lost social virtue – a set of firmly held beliefs arose that provided the ideological framework of the revival. And it's also natural that, as this frame of reference became the *raison d'être* of the timber frame revival, a selective cross-section of the history of timber construction was marshaled in support of the movement. The resulting ideas have persisted to the present day as a kind of dogma, fostering both the romance and appeal of the timber frame as well as an arguably specious hierarchy of authenticity.

First and foremost among these ideas has been the belief that the only *genuine* timber frame is a whole-house timber frame. As timber frame revivalists looked to the lessons of the past, the early Americans' dwellings and barns constructed entirely with heavy timbers – with their fascinating and ingenious joinery, their rich patinas, and aesthetic seductiveness – became the inspiring paradigm and the touchstone of authenticity.

In this view, to embrace the combination of construction materials and methods in a hybridized building approached sacrilege. But the main ideological problem arising from the commingling of timber framing with conventional contemporary building methods is not so much the mere fact that building methods and materials are being mixed. Indeed, other past hybrid construction technologies have been accorded the status of authenticity. It's much more the case that in a typical timber frame and stud-wall hybrid a building method such as timber framing – invested with all the cachet and nostalgia for noble lost forms – has been interbred with a building method often considered the bastard step-child of the industrial revolution, the upstart that disrupted the idyll of our past authentic sense of dwelling.

These firmly held attitudes and prejudices have begun to fade in the face of changes in thinking about the built environment. At the forefront of these changes is the growing concern for man's impact on the environment. If we are to sustainably harvest the timber resources needed for our industry, then their use should be maximized in areas of structural and aesthetic significance. Among timber framers, a wider acceptance of the ability of modern conventional building methods to provide effective solutions for age-old problems of shelter – moisture and humidity, air infiltration, and insulation against heat and cold, in a word, *comfort* – has also contributed to a gradual erosion of these prejudices. Finally, as the aesthetic of timbered structures has gained greater popularity, the attitudes and values of the traditionalist have been increasingly submerged by the expanding use of the craft in its effort to satisfy a growing clientele. Some staunch traditionalists, to their credit, rightly maintain that the agenda of preservation and revival of the past is in fact advanced by the vitality – even the commercialization – of the timber frame industry and the expansion of its appeal to mainstream middle-class society.

If the history of humankind's search for shelter is a reliable guide, then, in the final analysis, authenticity in our methods of constructing shelter must be defined in terms of present realities – realities of natural resources and economy, of social environment and cultural norms. For early man, these realities were fixed within a closely defined set of conditions. The question of authenticity could have never arisen – shelter took shape out of whatever materials and technologies were available.

In early historical times, the construction methods of shelter were similarly defined by present material realities, even while the constraints of those realities had begun to loosen and expand with man's mastery over his environment. The architectural opulence of high Greek, Roman, and Gothic civilization – while appearing to transcend the constraints governing the construction of shelter – was equally conditioned by religious, cultural, and socio-political realities. Even at this early date, as we have seen in our historical survey of timber construction, man's yearning for earlier innocence and authenticity found expression in the architectural reinterpretations of past methods and materials. Authenticity and reverence for the past has ever since been a primary concern of the builder and architect, although it has often been redefined according to historic conditions. A common thread through these many redefinitions has been their retrospective character.

In the late nineteenth and early twentieth centuries the idea that "form follows function" took firm root in architectural thinking. According to this idea, the *form* of any object of utility – the aesthetic character of that object, be it a house, a piece of furniture, an appliance – must be determined by the object's *function*. Embellishing the object in a way that unnecessarily adds to the object is to be dishonest. Like any great idea, the notion that form must follow function has stimulated a lively debate. It has been countered that a wide variety of forms is available to effectively satisfy the functional requirements of any object, architectural or otherwise. A house can give us shelter in an infinite number of ways. A judgment of authenticity or design integrity, in other words, cannot look to how well a particular form accords with its function, since many forms can accomplish the same thing.

In timber framing, even if we assume an ideal convergence of form and function, this idea does not support the prejudices that rank the "full house" timber frame over its hybridized form. Consider, once again, the challenges facing early American timber framers. The timber frame we have come to know from our books and magazines shows a surprising weakness in the face of lateral loads – the sideways push of the wind against the walls of a structure. In the teeth of a gale, even the stoutest of early American timber frame dwellings would have raised a cacophony of creaks, howls, and sharp reports. The hulking New England barns at times resorted to massive stone gable end walls to handle these loads, or to a proliferation of long braces, straining from the floor up to the tops of a post, from the beams overhead down to the floor, or crisscrossing the roof timbers in a riot of triangulation. Once bisected and trisected in this manner, the interior space of these structures loses much of the cavernous, open-plan character prized in contemporary timber frame great rooms, not to mention posing the threat of an epidemic of bruised shins and bashed noggins. Lovers of timber-framed barns converted into homes have been known to hack away at critical structural members in a misguided effort to render these spaces palatable to contemporary notions of interior design.

The modern timber frame hybrid responds to our needs, values, and aspirations in an often elegant synthesis of contemporary and traditional construction technologies, tempered by the patterns of dwelling to which we are accustomed. Whereas the whole-house timber frame – unaided by modern building methods – often requires extraordinary measures to handle lateral loads, the hybrid relies on exterior stud framing or structural insulating panels to do that work. Where the former consumes vast quantities of raw materials, fabrication time, and financial resources, the latter makes economical and ecologically responsible use of these. And where the former demands often complex and costly strategies to handle modern conveniences and comforts such as plumbing, electricity, heat, and ventilation, the latter simply avails itself of techniques in every builder's tool bag. The timber frame hybrid only asks that we relinquish the functionally redundant, as well as our preconceptions and misguided notions about this enduring and captivating means of expressing an elemental sense of dwelling.

Ludwig Mies van der Rohe – one of the giants of modernist architecture – famously proclaimed that "less is more," a rallying cry against the gaudy excesses of the neo-classical tradition. The generations-long battle waged over the marriage of form and function resonates in this axiom, and has often led to the creation of abstract and austere – at times even sterile – architectural statements. In the seemingly remote province of the modern timber frame, however, the streamlined and rational approach of the hybrid accords well with the contemporary realities of crafting dwellings – in aesthetics, economy, and ecology – while *concentrating* rather than overstating the expression of humankind's fundamental experience of dwelling. To maintain that this expression is somehow inferior to or less authentic than the traditionalistic whole house timber frame is to submit blindly to a self-deluding ideology.

THE RANGE OF CHOICES

Not every reader, no doubt, needs to be propelled toward the choice of a hybrid timber frame with quite the historical and philosophical force we have tried to marshal here. For whatever the reason, that choice may already have been made. Perhaps in your case there is much more a concern that the choices in a hybrid timber frame may be limited. Rest assured: you're more likely to end up agonizing over the sheer embarrassment of choices with which you're about to be faced.

To illustrate the depth and breadth of the possibilities available, let's take a hypothetical case. Say you have a room in mind; say it's an addition to an existing home or an area in a home that you would like to build. Call it a living room, a recreation room, a keeping or great or gathering room or what you will. Now let's give it a footprint of, say, 20 feet by 32 feet. Just to reign things a bit, let's limit the room to a single storey, although that storey can be anywhere from 8 feet to 12 feet high at the eaves. Now let's make the roof a relatively steep 12:12 pitch (that's a 45° angle, or 12" of rise for every 12" of run). And finally, let's run the ridge of the roof in the 32-foot direction. There – we've narrowed it down quite a bit. Or have we?

The first three figures illustrate full room timber frames (not a ***full house*** frame, unless you're planning to live in a single room). In these designs the timbers are doing all the work of supporting the weight of the roof and transferring that load to the foundation. The frame design in figure (1) uses "minor purlins" to span the distance between the "principle rafters." Purlins are timbers that run parallel to the ridge beam and the eaves spanning the space between the principle rafters, and they are intended to provide support for the materials that make up the roof. Principle rafters are the heavy, load-bearing rafters that make up the trusses, or "bents," in a timber frame.

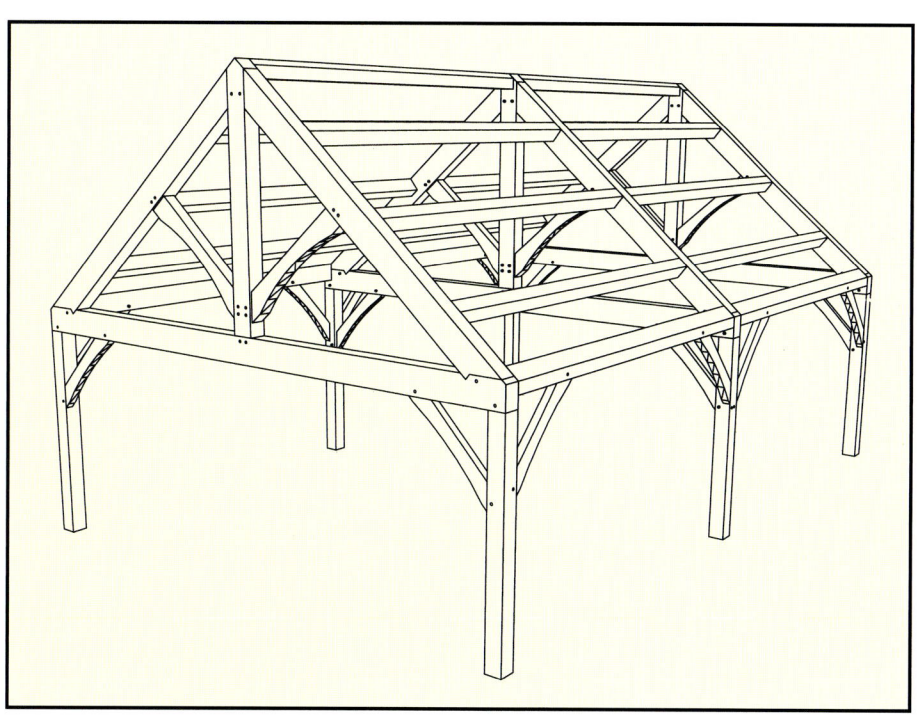

Figure 1. Full frame: 3 bents, 2 bays with purlins – 56 timbers

In many contemporary and historical timber frames, the roof begins with boards – barn boards, fresh-milled white pine tongue and groove, or the like – attached to the purlins, running from the eaves up to the ridge beam. Figures (2) and (3) illustrate a different approach to the roof timbers, with "principle rafters" and "common rafters" instead of purlins providing the support for roof materials. Common rafters are generally smaller in cross section than the principle rafters of trusses, and usually there are more of them. Where a principle rafter might be an 8 x 12 or larger timber, a common rafter is likely to be only a 4 x 12. In a rafter configuration, the roof boards run horizontally, parallel to the ridge and eaves.

Despite their obvious differences, all three of these frame designs are similar in that they consist of three bents with the spaces between the bents being spanned or filled in with purlins or rafters to support the roof. They all use braced posts to provide support for the roof structure, and every exterior plane of the room is defined by timbers.

The frame shown in figure (3), however, has 68 timbers, while the frame in figure (1) has only 56. Because every timber added to a frame has to be carved and joined to other timbers, the cost of timber framing is often closely tied to the **number** of timbers in a frame. It should come as no surprise then that one of the key strategies in making the beauty of heavy timbers more affordable is to find ways of reducing the frame's density and of minimizing structural redundancy.

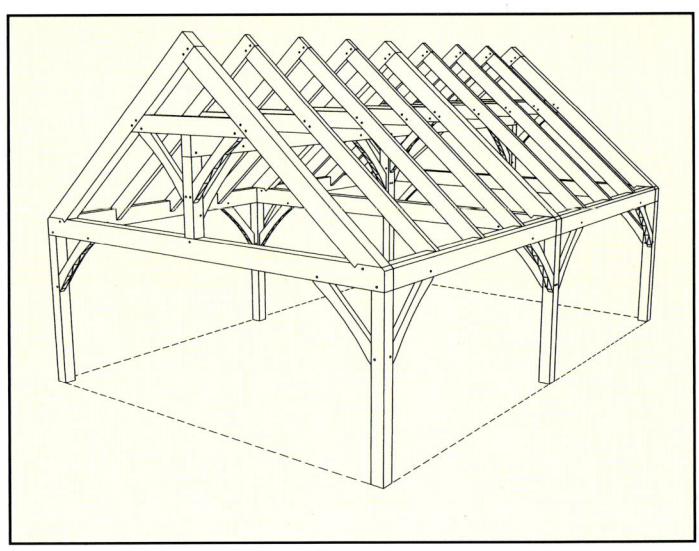

Figure 3. Full frame: 3 crown post trusses, 2 bays with common rafters – 68 timbers

The following figures illustrate how many possibilities there are to accomplish this, and what some of those solutions would look like. In figures (4) and (5) the frame designs previously illustrated are modified to eliminate the end bents, integrating the timber frame with the end walls, which could be stud or panel walls. In these designs, the conventionally framed end walls do some of the work that the timber posts did in the earlier designs, but at a lesser cost. The overall appearance hasn't changed that much, though. There are just as many purlins or rafters in these designs, and there are still posts and braces. A single bent has been eliminated in each of these designs, and the remaining two bents moved in toward the center of the room. The design illustrated in figure (4) has eliminated 15 of the most labor-intensive timbers from the design in figure (1). The frame shown in figure (5) has fared equally well, trimming 15 timbers from the design in figure (3). That's a good start.

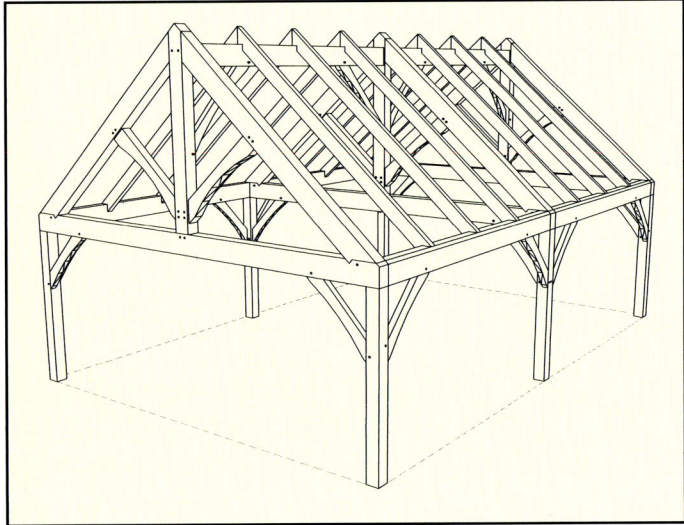

Figure 2. Full frame: 3 bents, 2 bays, with common rafters – 60 timbers

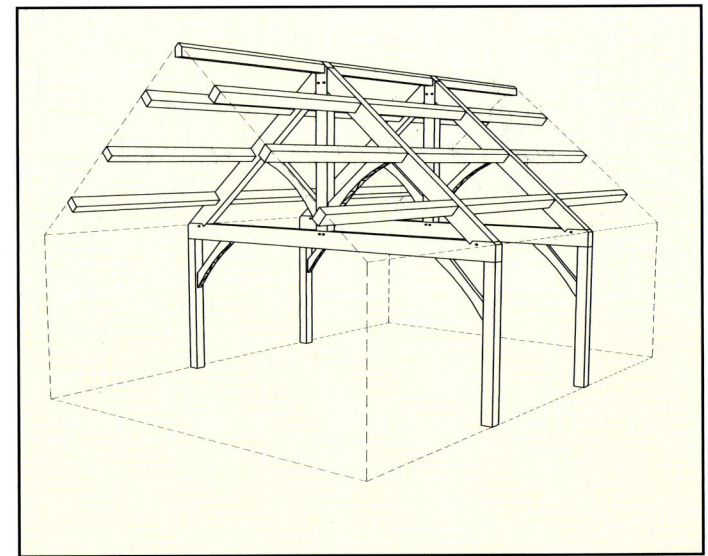

Figure 4. 2 trusses, 3 bays with purlins – 41 timbers

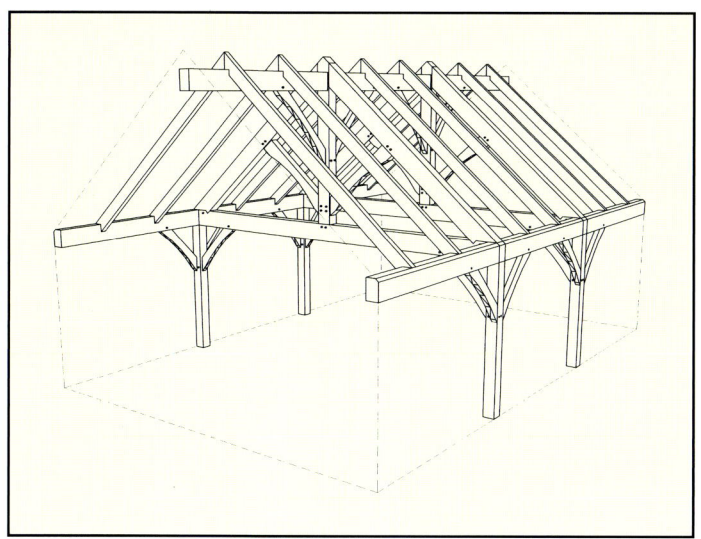

Figure 5. 2 Bents, 3 bays with common rafters – 53 timbers

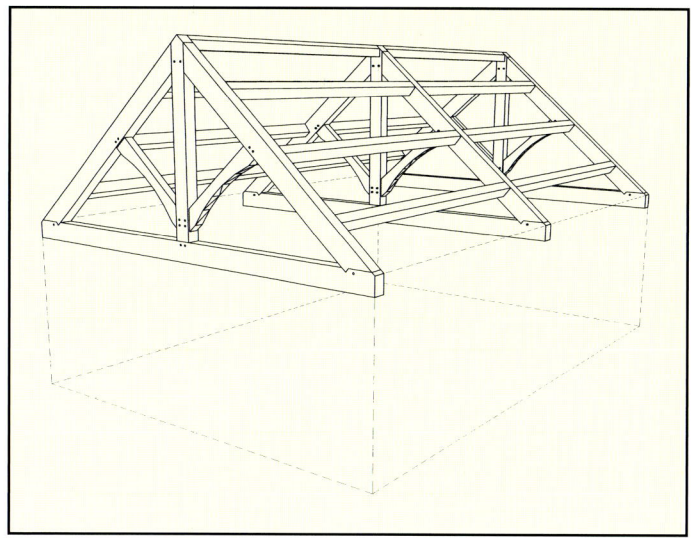

Figure 6. 3 Trusses, 2 bays with purlins – 32 timbers

We don't have to stop here, though. Even if we keep almost all the roof timbers from the design illustrated in figure (1), we can begin to achieve an even more significant reduction in the number of timbers by eliminating the posts and their braces and eave plates. (Eave plates are the horizontal timbers – parallel to the purlins and the ridge – that define the change in direction from the pitch of the roof to the verticality of the walls.) Sure, having all those posts and braces appeals to some timber frame enthusiasts, but in many cases they're not actually necessary from a structural point of view. From the perspective of interior design, they can also be a problem, since window layout and furniture arrangements can be more challenging when trying to work around all those posts and braces.

So let's see what happens when we take out the posts. The three trusses in figure (6) rest on top of stud walls and are connected by purlins and ridge beams just as in the design in figure (1). The end trusses still rest against the gable end walls. The design in figure (7) eliminates one of the trusses, and has the purlins resting on the gable end walls. We've eliminated one of the bents, but there's another bay now, so the design in figure (7) actually has one more timber than the one illustrated in figure (6). Purlins are easier and faster to carve than whole trusses, though, so the latter design could well work out to be a little less expensive. These changes alone would significantly reduce the cost of the timber frame compared with the frames shown in the first three drawings.

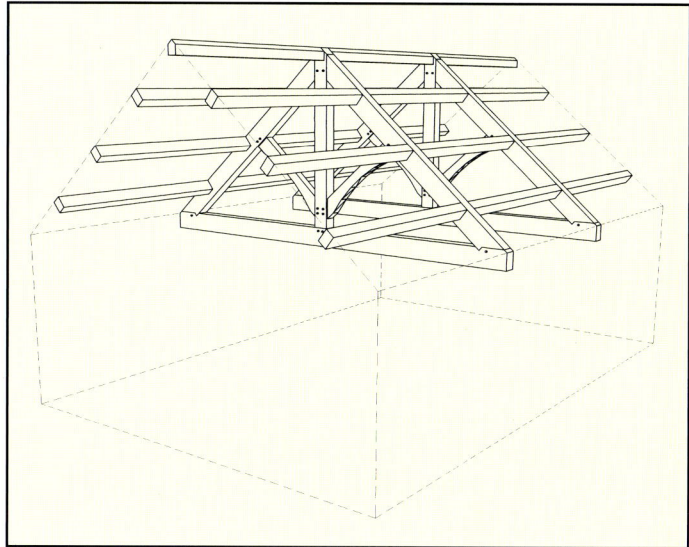

Figure 7. 2 Trusses, 3 bays with purlins – 33 timbers

If you were so inclined, you could save even more by trimming the frame down to its bare bones. In figure (8) we've taken out yet another truss, ending up with a single one in the middle of the room. From a high count of 68 timbers, we're now down to a mere 20. Admittedly this configuration is a bit lean, but for some of you it may be just enough to bring the warmth and visual interest of heavy timbers into a home.

One could also just as easily *increase* the density of the frame, keeping three trusses but moving them in – as in figure (9) – from the gable end walls and pocketing an extra set of purlins into the conventionally framed end walls. Now the timber count has climbed back up to 46, but, again, they're the smaller, relatively simple purlins that have been added. This frame design would certainly be visually imposing, perhaps even a bit busy and over-bearing for some tastes.

Taking a hard look at the timber frame design and looking for ways to eliminate frame components isn't driven entirely by the construction budget. Hybridizing a timber-framed house in this manner also often helps to solve problems of interior design. For example, in the designs shown in figures (7) through (9), moving the trusses in and away from the end walls has the added benefit of allowing more flexibility with window placement at the gable ends.

The timber frames illustrated in figures (4) through (9) are all variations of the first frame in the series. The same exercise could be performed with the rafter system frame illustrated in figure (2), eliminating and substituting timbers in order to pare down the elements that drive the cost of the frame. The example in figure (10) takes the frame design from figure (2) and removes the structurally redundant posts, braces, and eave plates, just as we did earlier with the purlin system frame. This simplification takes the timber count from 60 down to 32, again a savings of almost half. The designs in figures (11) to (13) carry the process even further, reducing a bit here, and adding a bit there, with the last frame in the set reduced to an absolute minimum.

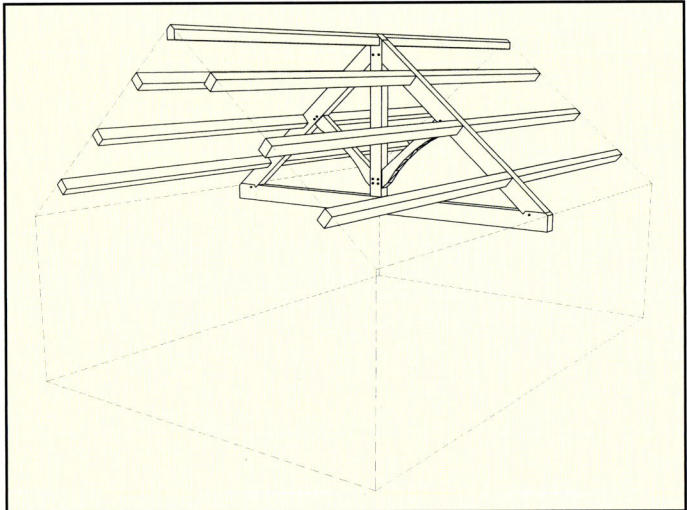

Figure 8. 1 Truss, 2 bays with purlins – 20 timbers

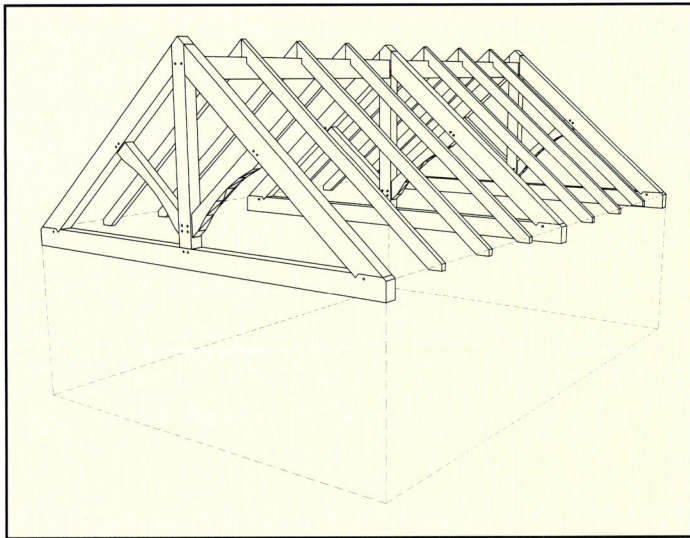

Figure 10. 3 Trusses, 2 bays with common rafters – 32 timbers

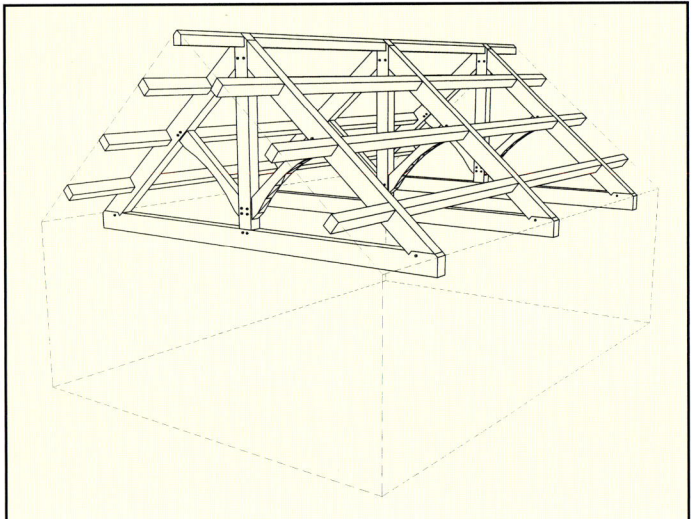

Figure 9. 3 Trusses, 4 bays with purlins – 46 timbers

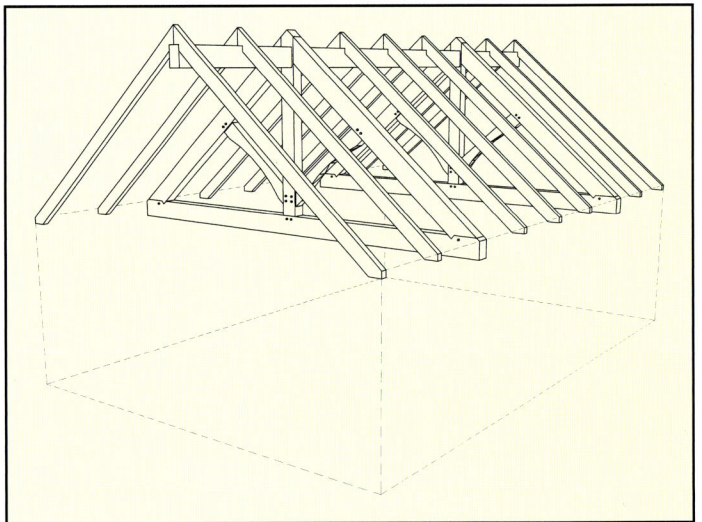

Figure 11. 2 Trusses, 3 bays with common rafters – 29 timbers

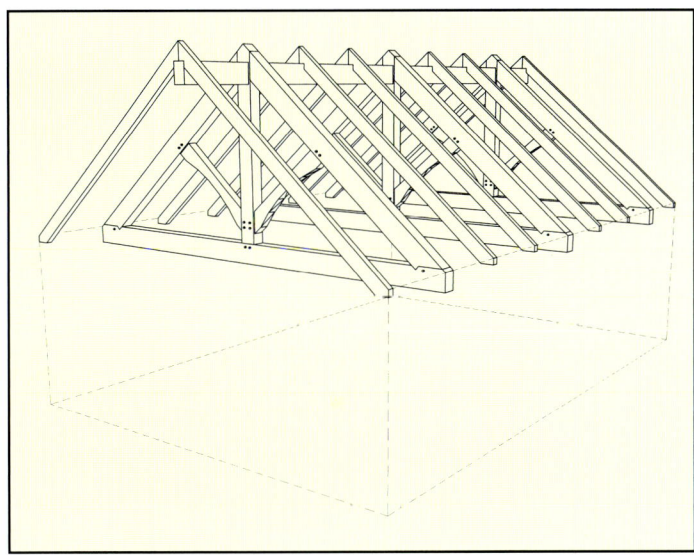

Figure 12. 3 Trusses, 4 bays with common rafters – 34 timbers

Many timber frame enthusiasts are captivated by the wide open spaces of contemporary timber frames, so for them these arrangements might not be the best choice. The frame configuration shown in figure (17) illustrates one possible solution, introducing a "bridge truss" to create a structural ridge. If one attempted to create a structural ridge with a single beam in this 32' long room, it would be a behemoth, 24" or more deep. A bridge truss is really nothing other than the old-fashioned timber railway structures as they were built in the early 1800s. Putting the structural workings of the timber frame on display like this is one of the primary urges of enthusiasts, and the bridge truss ridge satisfies that urge handsomely.

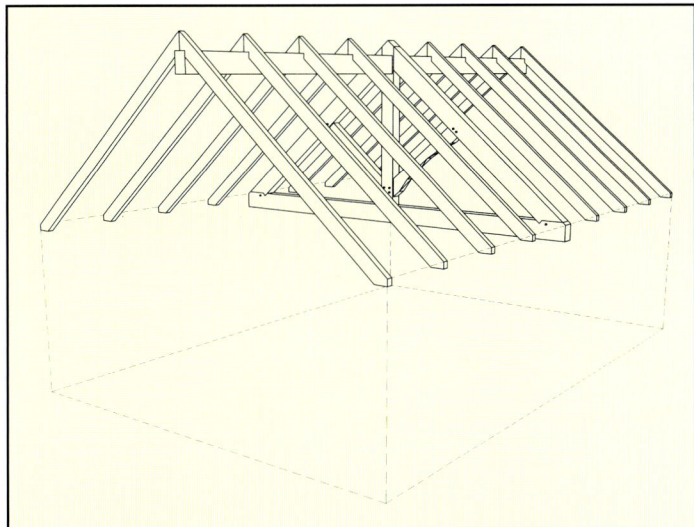

Figure 13. 1 Truss, 2 bays with common rafters – 24 timbers

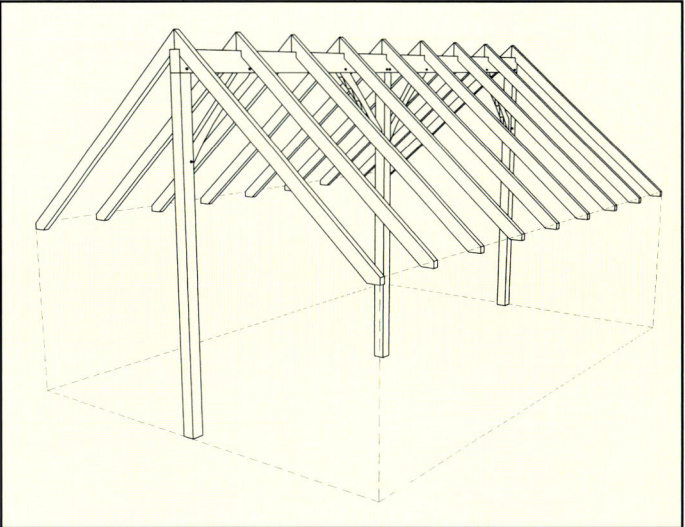

Figure 14. Structural ridge with 3 posts and common rafters – 26 timbers

Variation in timber frame design isn't just a matter of tweaking the frame a bit here or there. The rafter system design illustrated in figure (14) achieves an altogether different feel using a structural ridge supported by posts at the ends and the middle. Of course, a further reduction is possible by running the ends of the ridge beam into the conventionally framed end walls and eliminating the two end posts and their braces (figure 15). And now we might try replacing the ridge beam with two major purlins – ridge-like beams supporting rafters at the middle of their spans – and supported, in turn, by posts and braces at the middle of their spans (figure 16). These variants require interior posts to provide support for the ridge beam or major purlins.

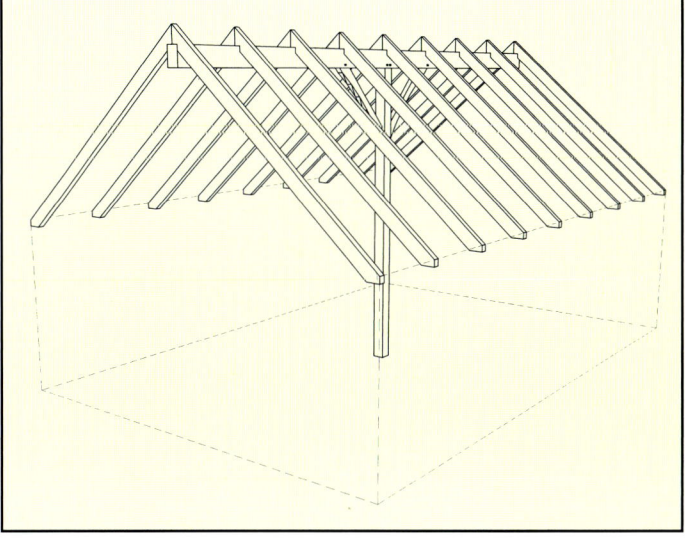

Figure 15. Structural ridge with 1 post and common rafters – 22 timbers

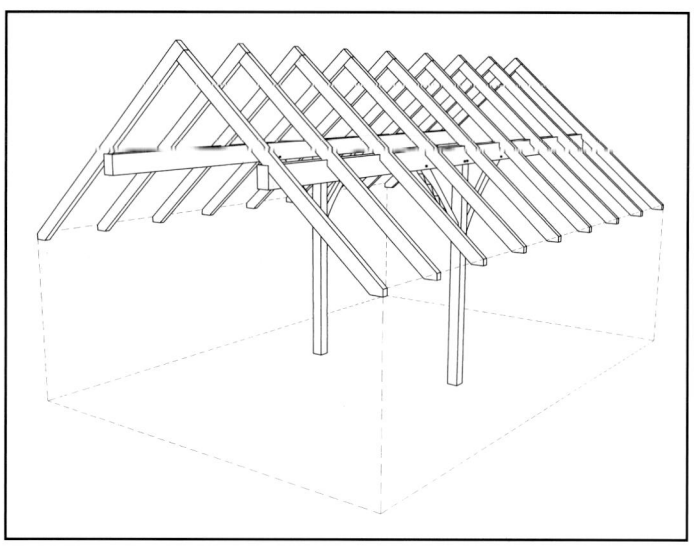

Figure 16. Common rafter system with major purlins – 26 timbers

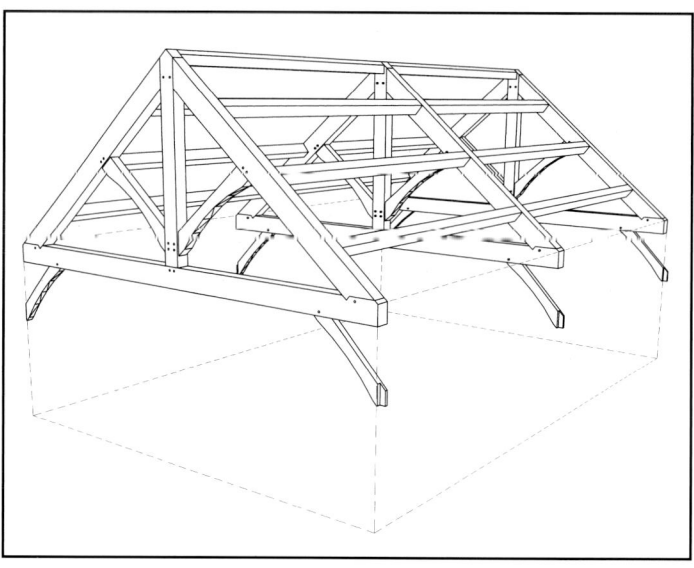

Figure 18. 3 Trusses, 2 bays with purlins and braces housed into stud walls – 38 timbers

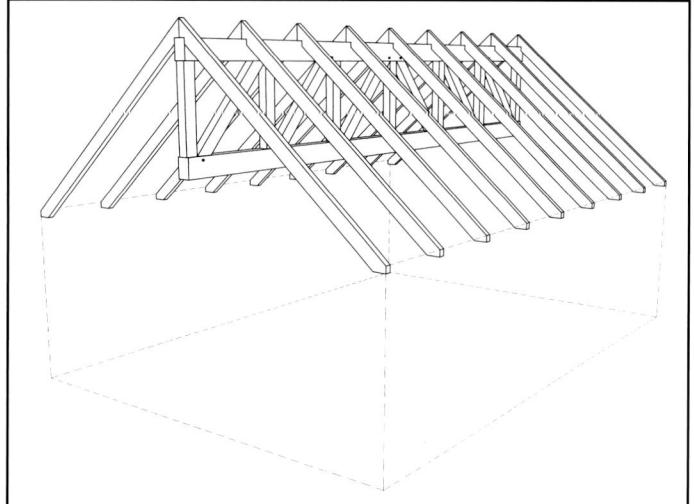

Figure 17. Common rafter system with bridge truss – 33 timbers

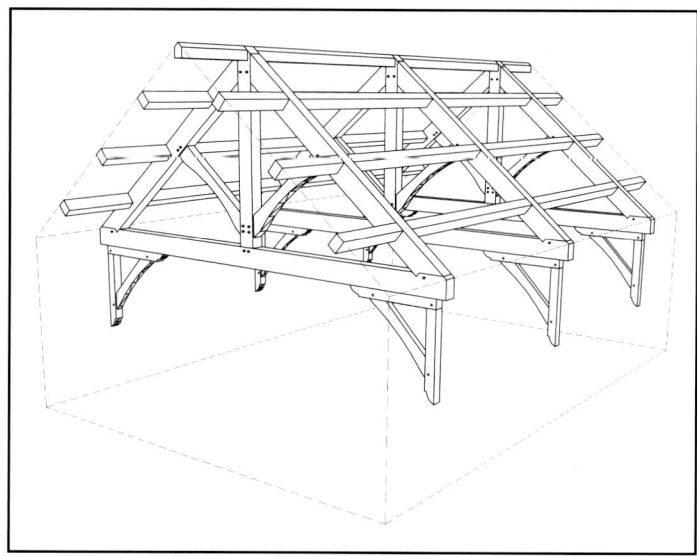

Figure 19. 3 Trusses, 4 bays with purlins and brackets – 64 timbers

These variations have concentrated on the functional aspects of timber frame design. Once we begin to embellish the frame, or to look for different frame configurations, the horizon opens wide. Consider the re-introduction of braces illustrated in figures (18) to (20). The first of these shows a fairly standard brace design, with the tenons at the toe of the braces pocketed into the stud wall much as they would join to posts. Figures (19) and (20) introduce a bracketed brace applied to both a purlin system and a rafter system. Braces provide a brilliant opportunity to embellish a frame. The many examples shown here (figures 21 and 22) represent a cross-section of the design possibilities and the various aesthetic sensibilities they can satisfy, from a plain barn-style brace to an ornately styled Victorian one.

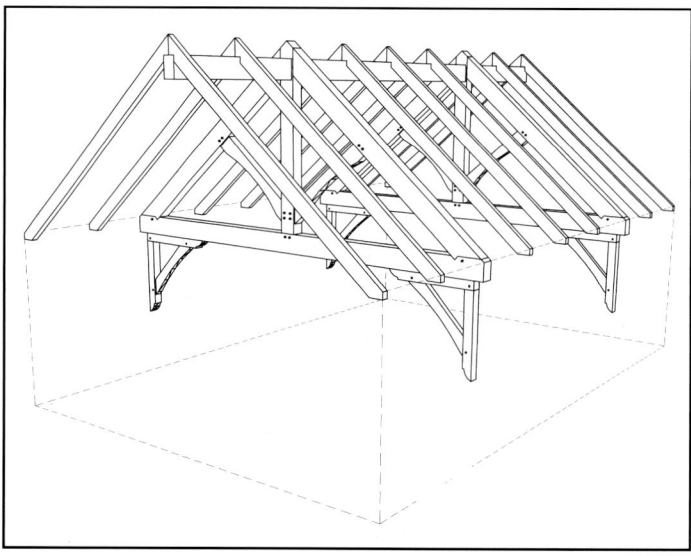

Figure 20. 2 Trusses, 3 bays with common rafters and brackets – 41 timbers

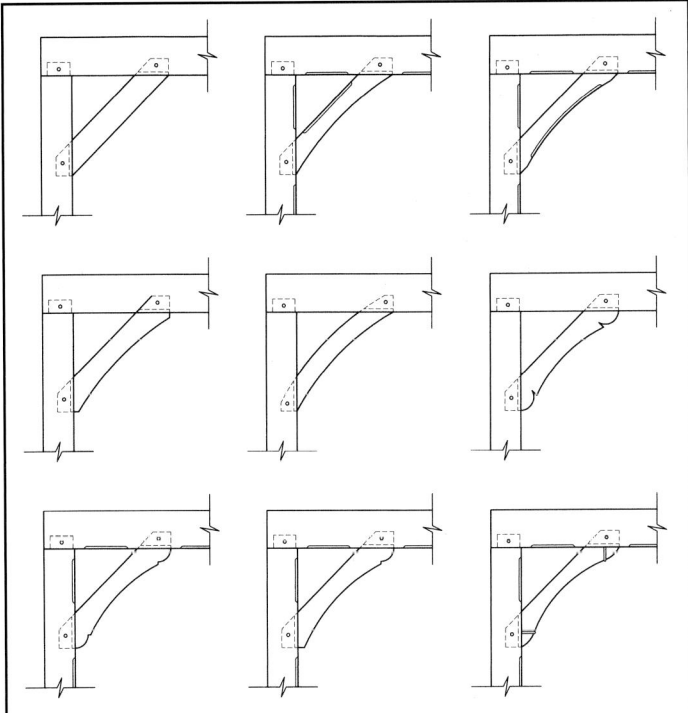

Figure 21.

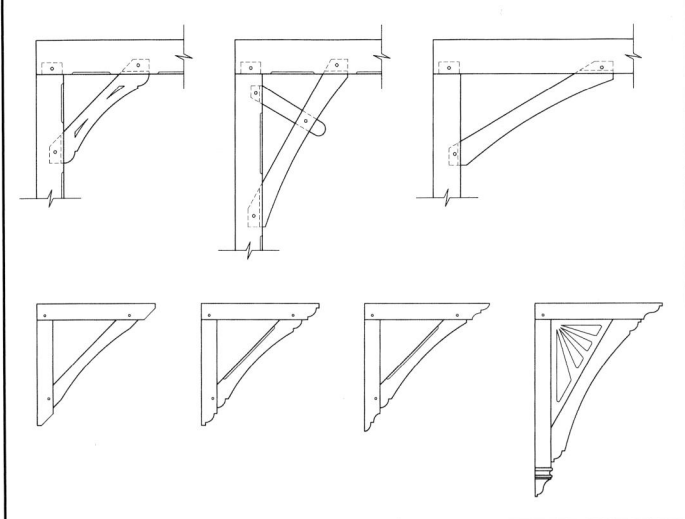

Figure 22.

At the heart of most of the frame designs we've looked at so far is the humble mainstay of timber framing, the strutted kingpost truss (figure 23). The kingpost itself is the vertical member in these frames and provides mid-span support for the "chord," the main horizontal member spanning from one wall to the other. This basic configuration has been around since the dawn of heavy timber construction, and has been endlessly modified and embellished. Just a few of the possibilities are shown in the following illustrations. Merely giving the struts – the diagonal bracing members – a slight curvature adds grace and elegance to a kingpost truss (figure 24), and adding an embellishment at the termination of the strut gives the frame a distinctly regional and historical flavor (figure 25).

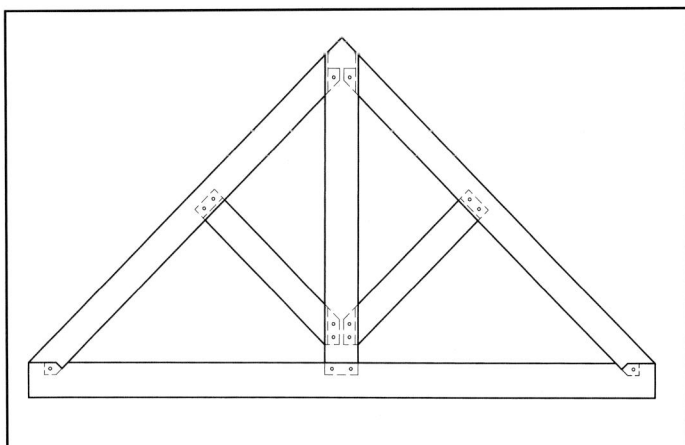

Figure 23.

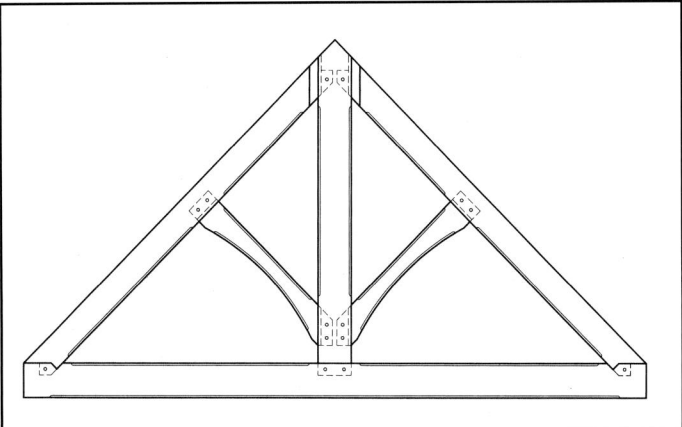

Figure 24.

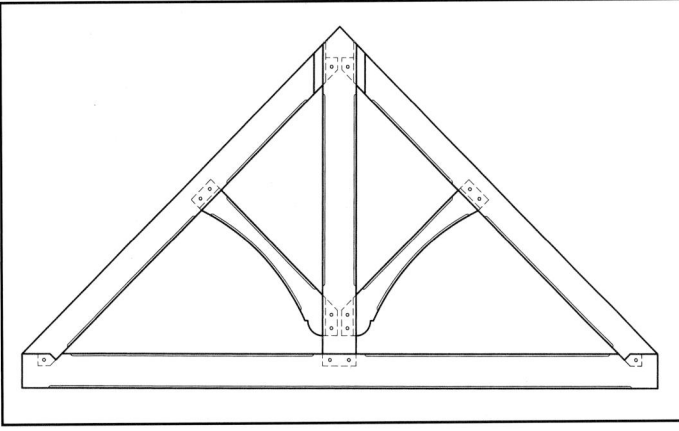

Figure 25.

41

Raising the chord of the truss as in figure (26) can enhance the feeling of loftiness in a living space, and helps to alter the overall scale of the timber truss relative to the space. The addition of bracing from the rafter ends up to the chord conveys a sense of robustness and can temper the severe geometry of the kingpost truss (figure 27). The two vertical members in the truss in figure (28) – "queenposts" – emphasize the utilitarian past of timber framing.

A single element of a frame can often be shaped and detailed in a variety of ways. The kingpost as a prominent component of many frame designs, for example, has been embellished in countless ways throughout history. A few of these possibilities are illustrated below in figure (29). The design ingenuity of past generations of timber framers has also contributed to a lexicon of timber embellishment. The through-tenon, illustrated in figure (30), enables the timber framer to use removable wedges to join individual timber members, but also showcases the marriage of form and function that is often associated with the timber frame. The kingpost and other similar frame members lend themselves well to lively displays of the impulse to ornament our homes. The old standby drop pendant termination of the kingpost in figure (31) is an example of a popular embellishment that might well have its roots in an early structural design solution. The acorn-shaped variant exemplifies the exuberance mentioned above.

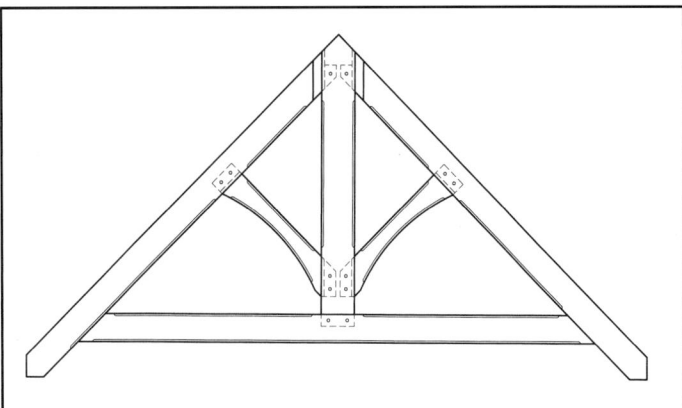

Figure 26.

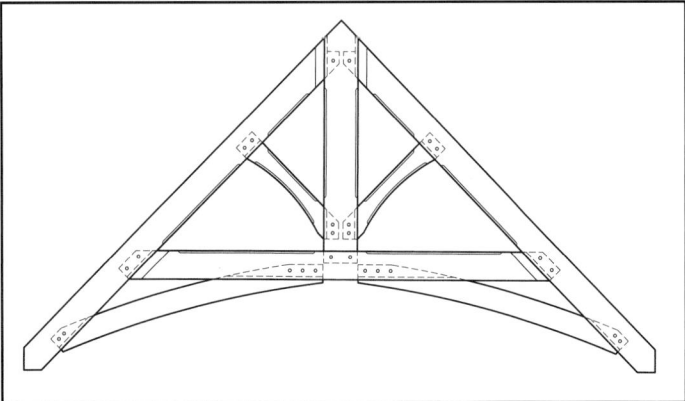

Figure 27.

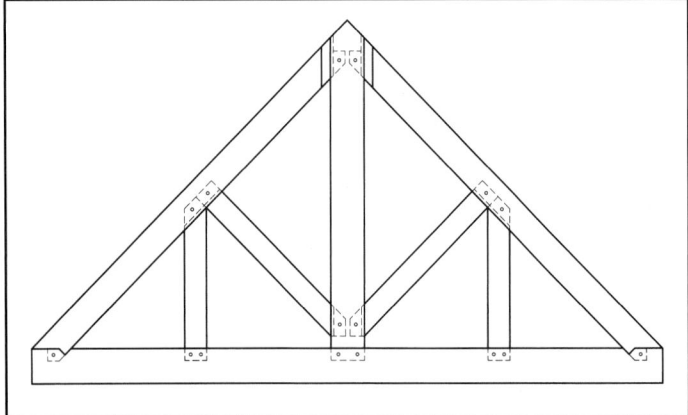

Figure 28.

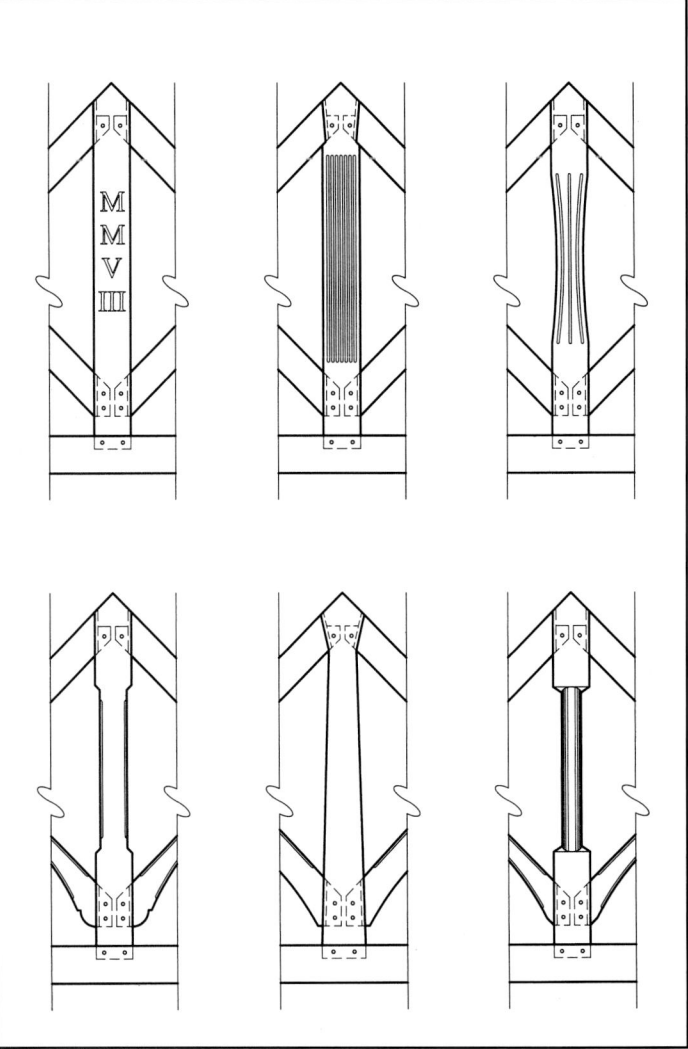

Figure 29.

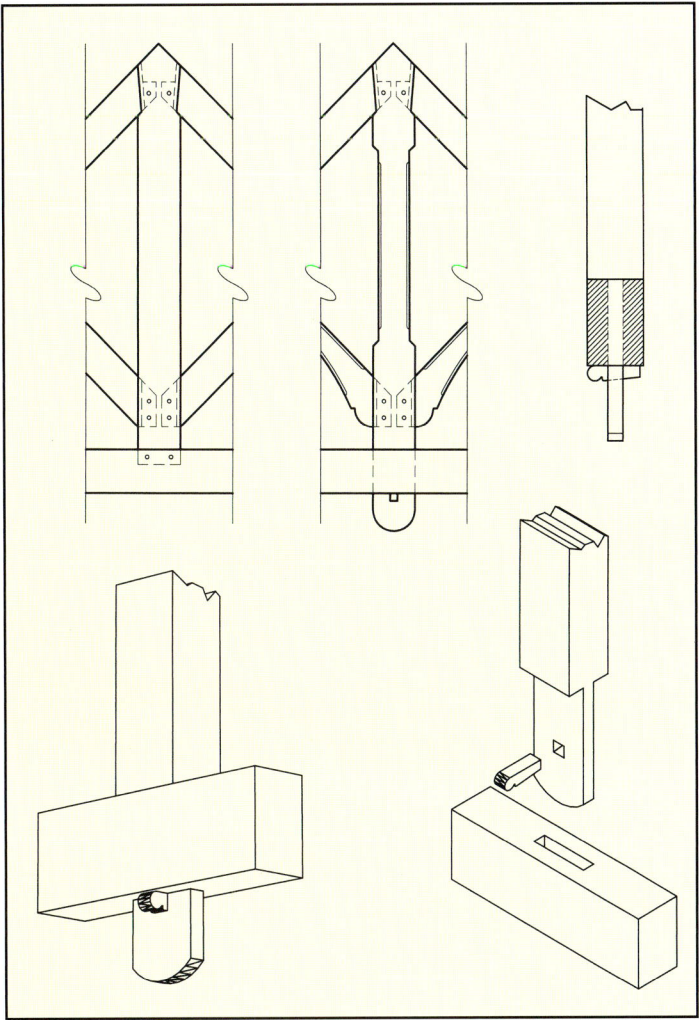

Figure 30.

Figure 30b.

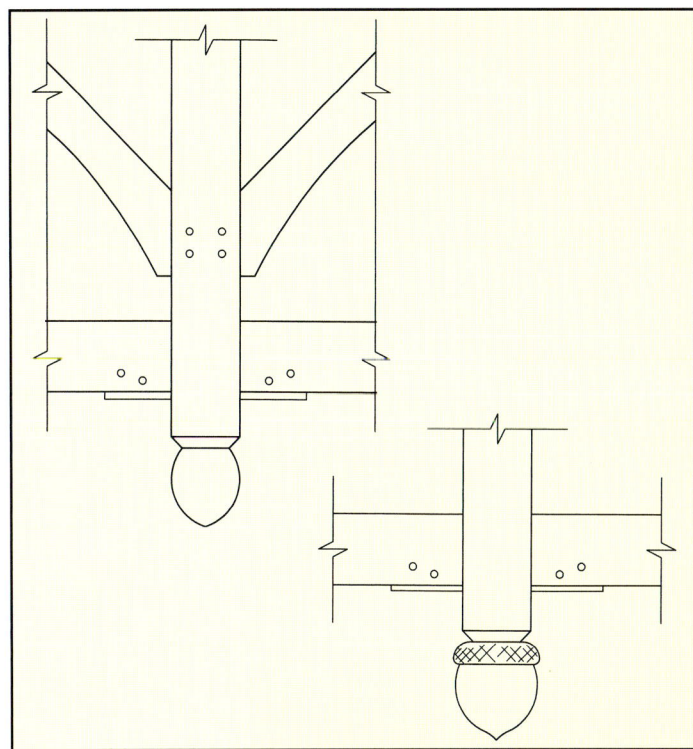

Figure 31.

Figure 31b.

Historical precedents are a fertile source of various methods for the embellishment and individualization of a timber frame. Steel plates and hardware strengthening the connections between members make a decisive graphical statement while playing a significant role in the structural system of a timber frame (figure 32). Modern building codes often require the addition of steel elements to help a structure handle extreme loads, and many a timber framer will make the extra effort to bury these elements inside the timbers in an attempt to preserve the "authentic" appearance of traditional timber joinery. Past generations of timber framers, however, made use of wrought iron structural reinforcement whenever design demanded and purses permitted it.

None of the options we've surveyed so far would force us to abandon any of the design parameters we started out with, either in regard to size or scope of hybridization. The kingpost truss has been the basis for most of the examples we've considered, but if that configuration doesn't satisfy one's aesthetic yearnings, there's still an abundance of other possible configurations.

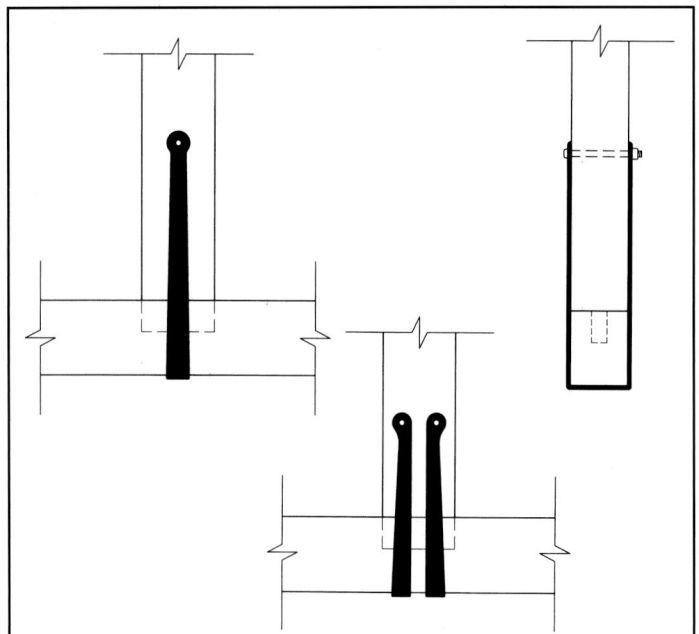

Figure 32.

be obvious by now just how vast the possibilities are, even though we started out with a tightly circumscribed set of parameters. Add a dormer or two, hips and valleys, a second level, or any of a host of other features, and the possibilities will seem infinite.

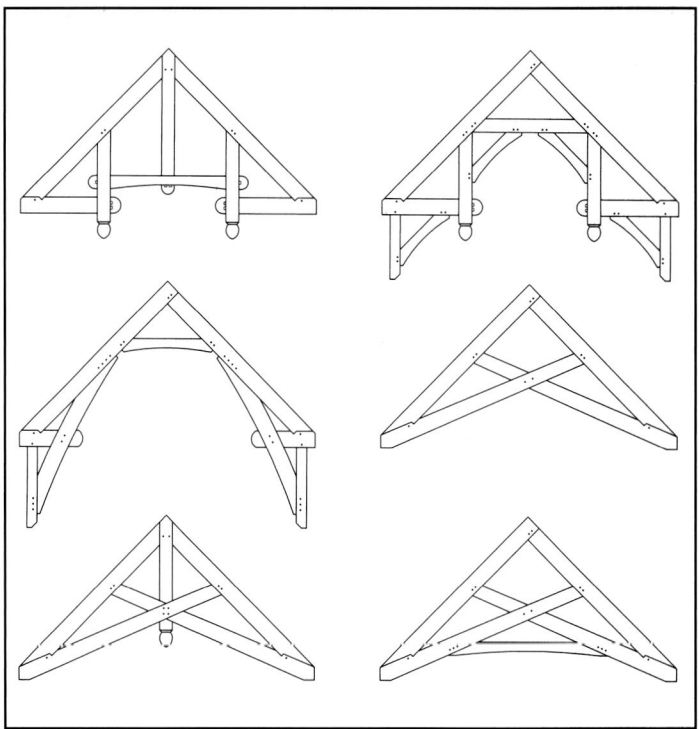

Figure 34.

The truss configurations below should begin to show the sheer volume of choices available (figures 33 and 34). And this is just the tip of the iceberg. Any one of these configurations could be found at the top of a list of other variants, simplifications, embellishments, and other hybridization strategies similar to the ones we've looked at above. Indulge us one final, extreme variation: consider the "cruck" type frame below (figure 35). As usual, this configuration itself is wide open to variation. So it should

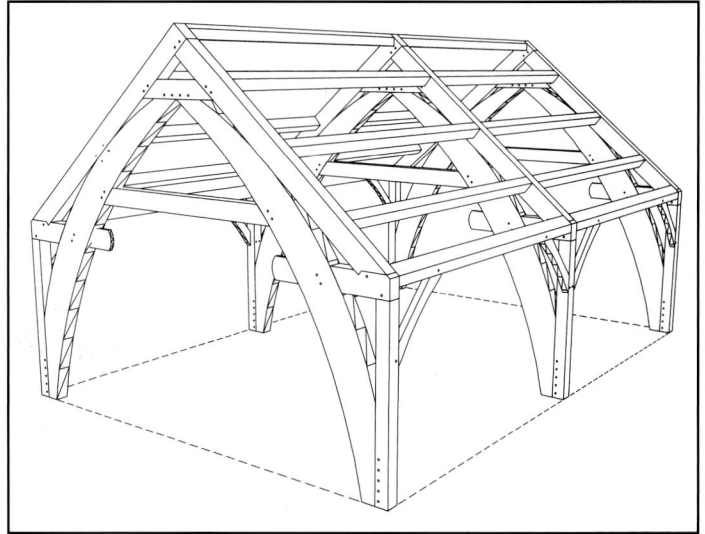

Figure 35. Full frame: 3 cruck trusses, 2 bays with purlins – 59 timbers

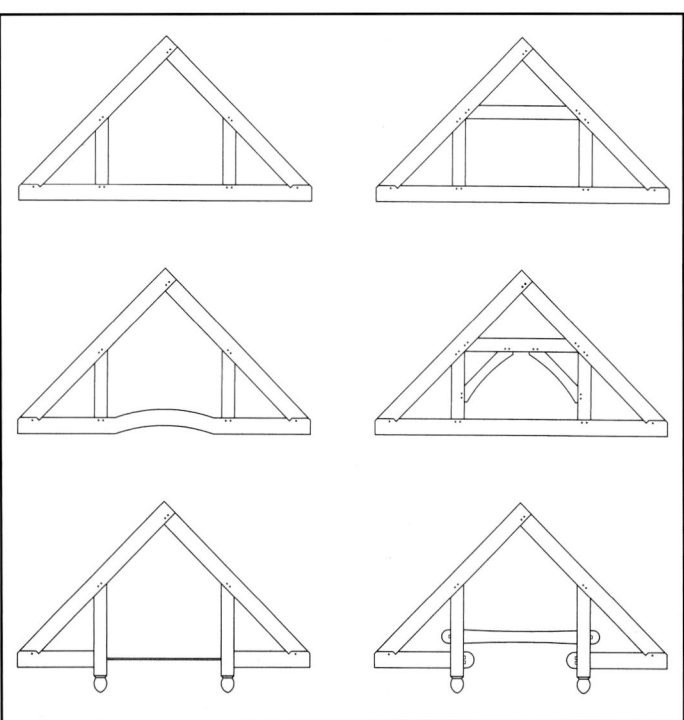

Figure 33.

A GALLERY OF
TIMBER FRAME HYBRIDS

This photographic essay of forty-two projects shows a wide range of approaches, of configurations, styles, surfaces, finishes, and budgets. Our intent was to showcase variety. None of the rooms were professionally furnished, staged, or decorated for our shoots. The photographs we took show the homes as our clients live in them.

In some cases clients came to us with very strong preferences; others gave us wider latitude. Some wanted multiple rooms timber framed; others wanted just one room, in one case simply a sheltered barbecue pit. Some sought a traditional feel; others opted for contemporary interpretations. Some were on tight budgets; for others the notion of monetary restraint seemed utterly foreign. All felt drawn, in some way, to the concept of structure and sculpture being one and the same.

Overlooking the Susquehanna River in York County, Pennsylvania, this hybrid has a timber framed great room topped by a cupola which pulls in light, a timber framed entrance, a timbered ceiling in the kitchen and dining room and posted girts that support a screened porch and a transition area between the house and garage. The timbers are Douglas fir. The house designer was Donald A. Dale, Inc.

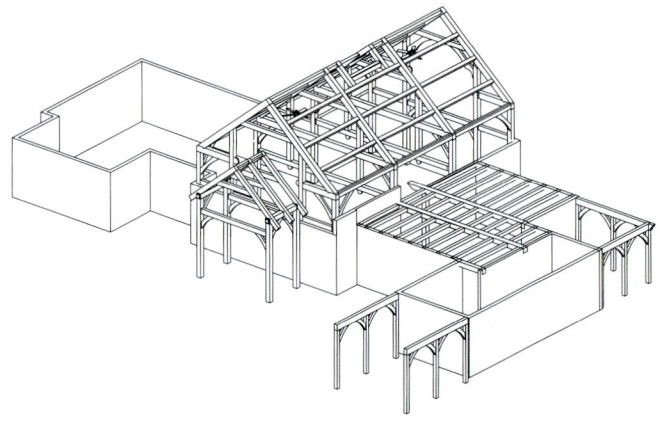

The owners loved their property and its location – Doylestown, Pennsylvania – but their small rancher seemed to compress in size with each passing year. The husband and architect Steve Thompson designed this solution. They lived in the rancher throughout the construction of the oak timber framed main section and the conventionally framed garage/design office. *Photographs courtesy of Steve Thompson.*

TAYLOR
CONTRACTORS
741-4432

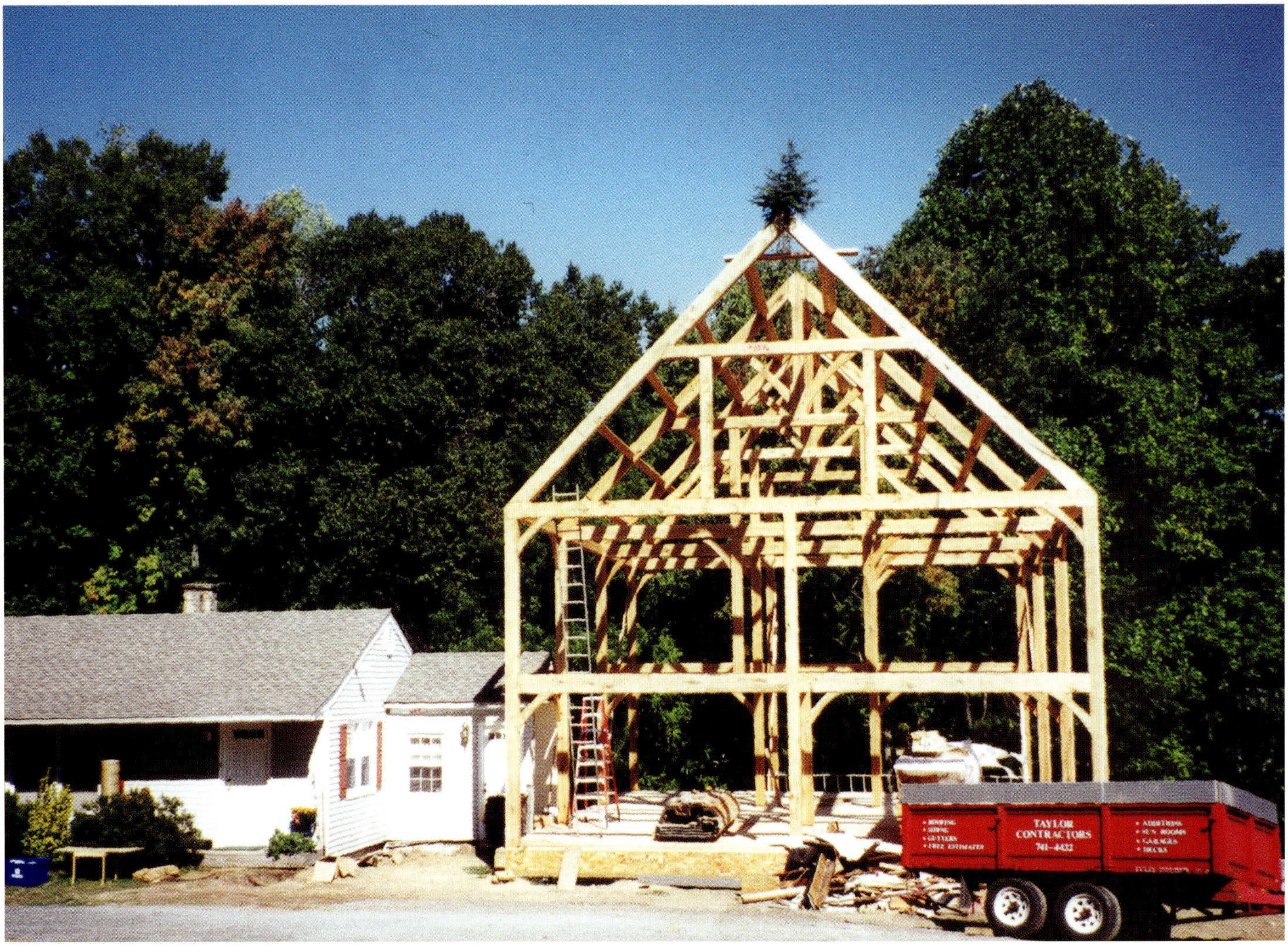

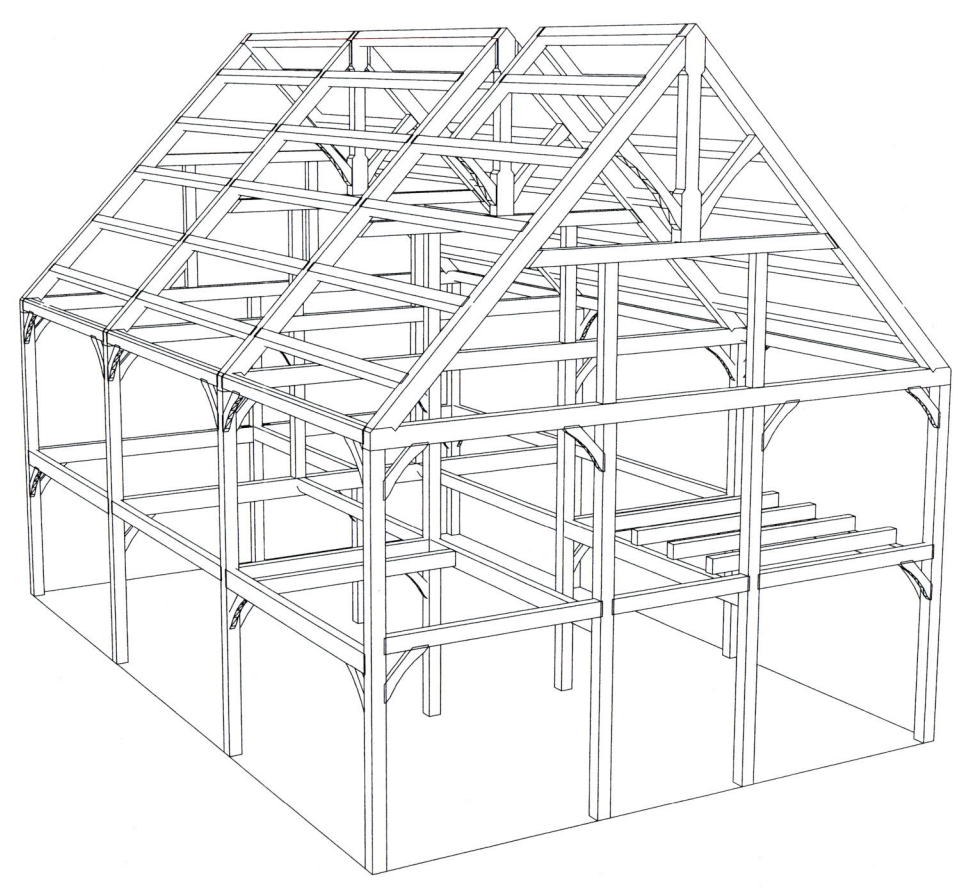

Gambrel timber frame trusses, by their very geometric nature, are difficult to configure if grace is part of the equation. The husband had told Zaya that LCTF, Inc. would get the contract if his design concept could make him wife smile. The use of arcs of the lower chords that gradually diminished in width as they moved towards the center had the desired effect. The ceiling boards and timber in this Long Island home are Douglas fir. The architect was Michael J. Wallin, Architect, PC.

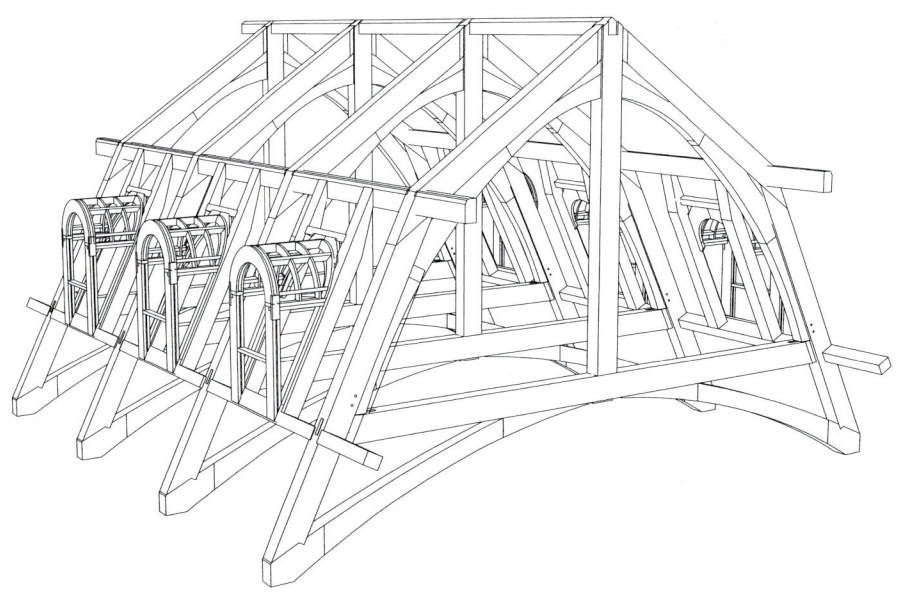

The timber frame pieces for this great room were fashioned from oak timbers from an old Pennsylvania barn and were not resurfaced. Trim in the great room and some of the adjacent areas were made from face cuts from some of the extra timbers. Home designer was Donald A. Dale, Inc.

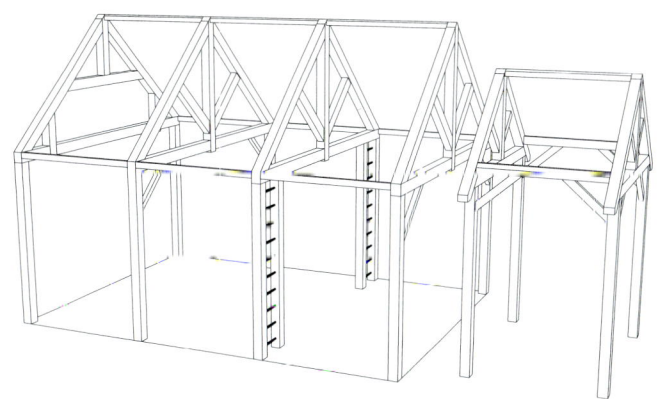

This stark and elegant Douglas fir frame outlines a kitchen addition for which the architect and builder, John Hubert Architects of Wyncote, Pennsylvania, won the Philadelphia Magazine Home & Garden Dream Kitchen/Contemporary Award in 2007. *Second photograph of kitchen courtesy of John Hubert.*

This four bent Douglas fir main section has a loft in one bay open to the kitchen, living, and dining areas. The master bedroom is under the loft. Design of this Central Pennsylvania house was by Lancaster County Timber Frames, Inc.

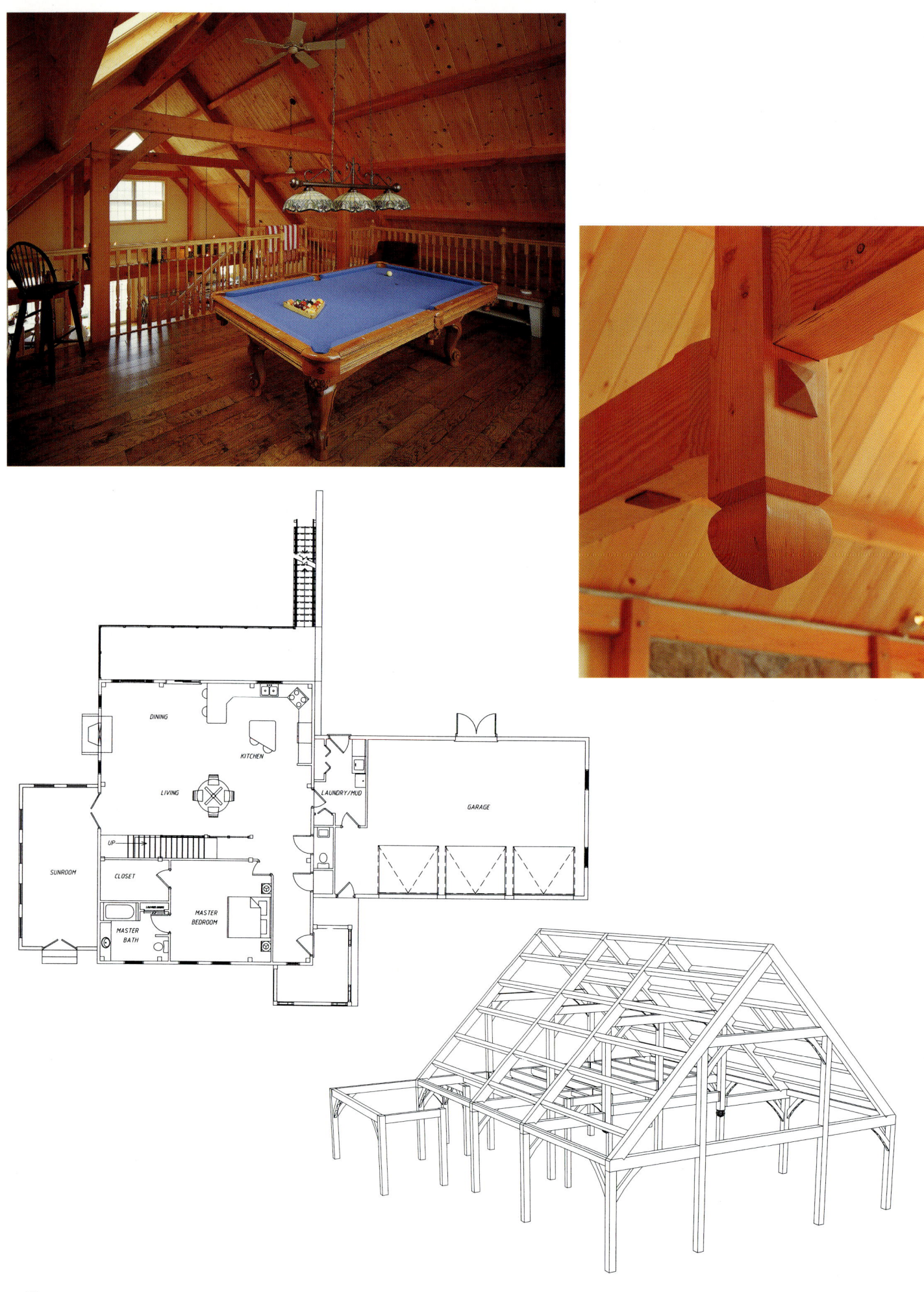

This Southeastern Pennsylvania home has a two story timber framed section. The first floor's great room and dining area are open to the top, while the kitchen is partially nestled below the second story bedrooms, which in turn have lofts above. The master suite, mudroom, and, of course, the garage are conventionally framed. The timbers are Douglas fir. Residential design was by Lancaster County Timber Frames, Inc.; the G.C. was Donald Banick, Builder.

Master Bathroom
Master Bedroom
Kitchen
Living Room
Hallway
Master Closet
Dining Room
Foyer
Laundry Room
Bath #1
Garage

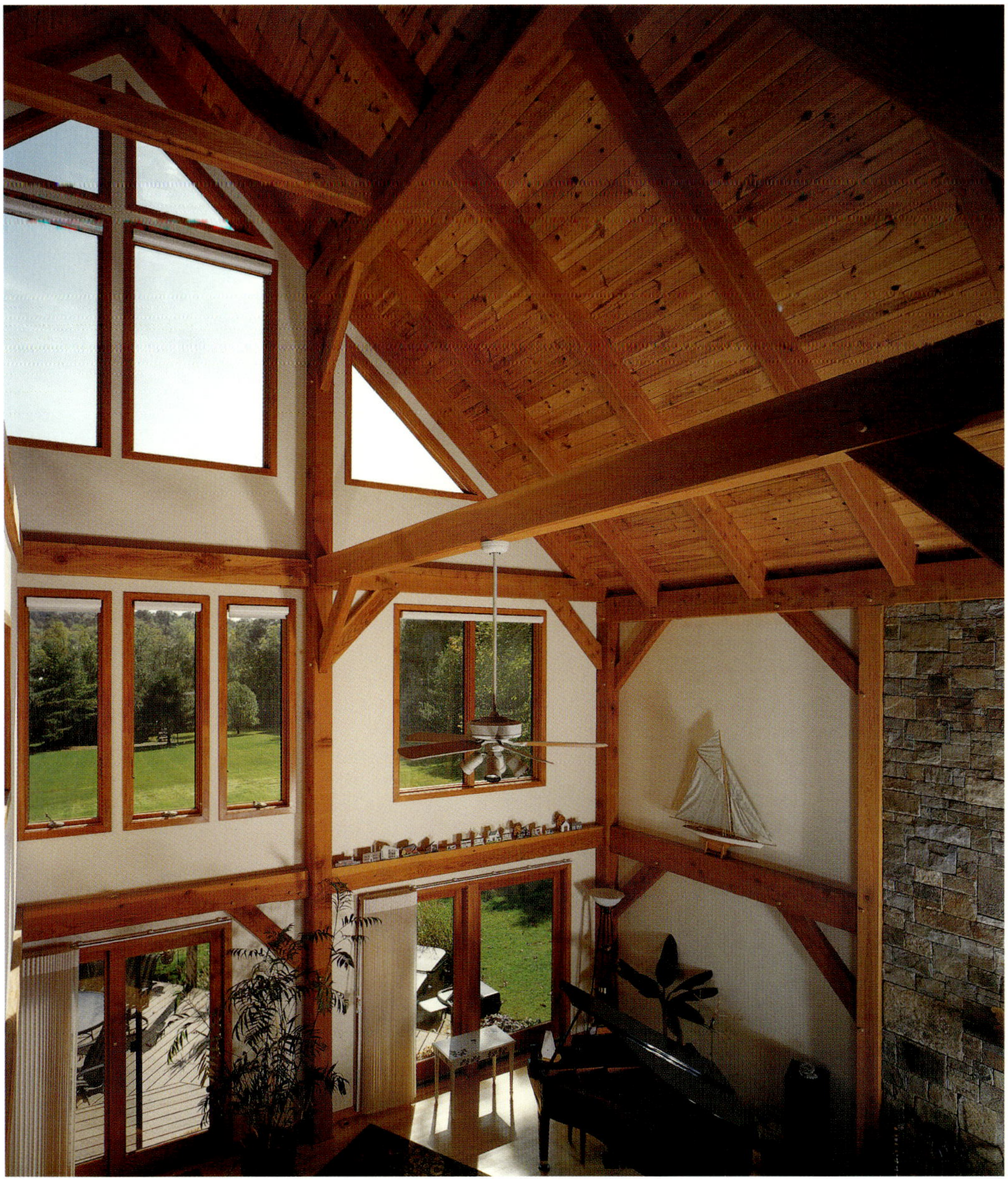

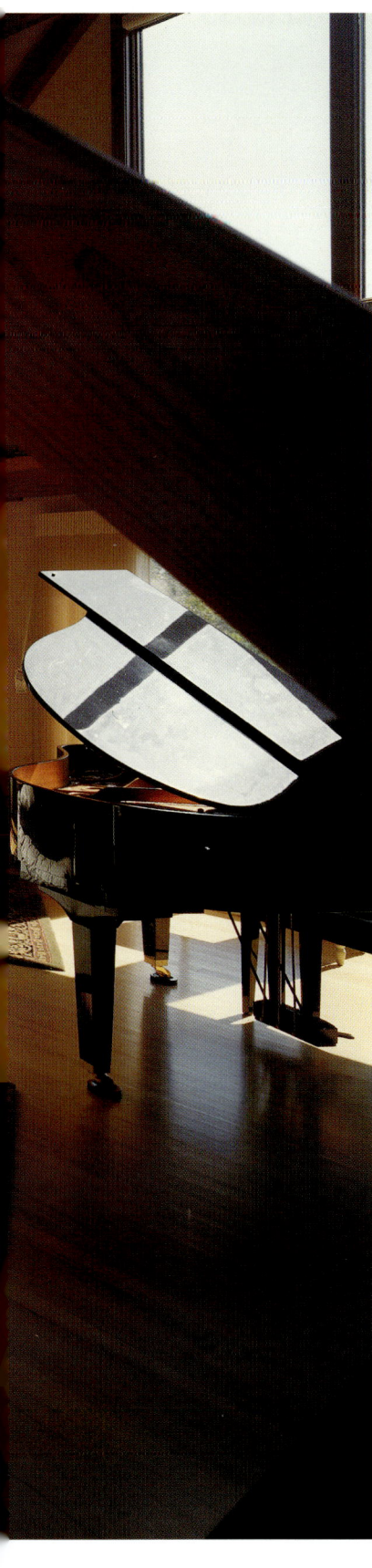

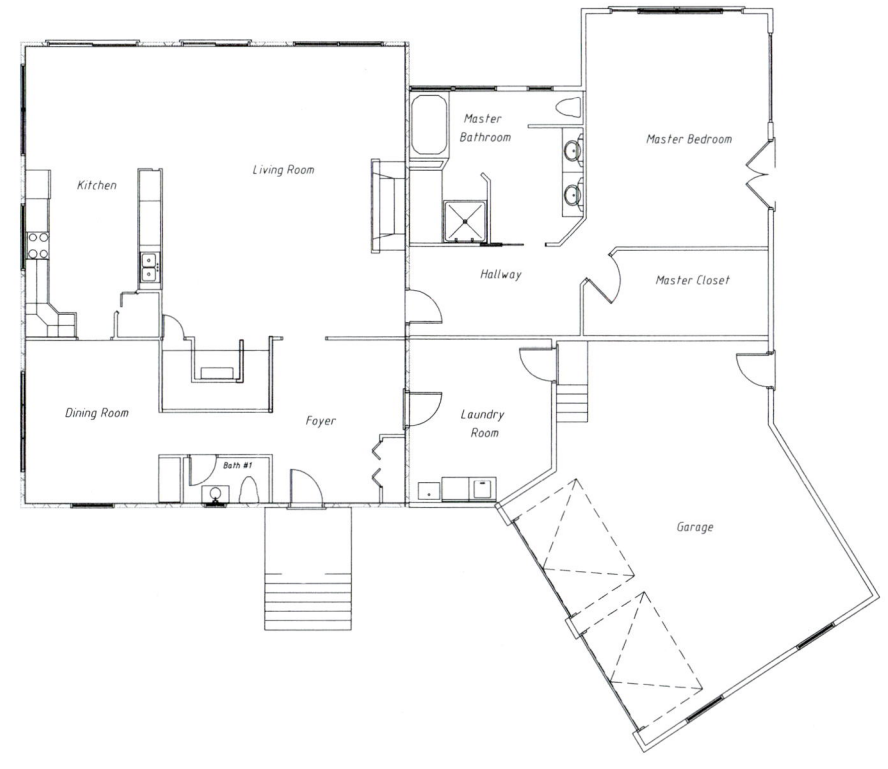

The owner of this Northern New Jersey home wanted a bit of an Old English feel. He inlayed the bricks between the dark stained oak timbers. It took him much longer than he believed it would.

This White Plains, New York, home has a painted mahogany porch, recycled long leaf yellow pine gathering room truss system and red oak trusses in the foyer. The G.C. was McKenna Custom Homes and the architect was Michael R. LaRocca, Ltd.
Photographs courtesy of Terry Lappe Olson of The Image Photographic Studio.

This stone house was built in 1797 in Chester County, Pennsylvania. The 26' by 30' Douglas fir timber frame, which was mated to it, features a whitewashed tongue and groove ceiling.

Located just outside of D.C., this home features a number of areas, both interior and exterior, that were framed from recycled rough cut Douglas fir timbers harvested from the original Marconi Wireless Factory. The architect, Scott Broughton of Colorado, brought a Northwestern feel to the project. The general contractor was Sandy Spring Builders, LLC. *Photographs courtesy of Scott Broughton.*

This Allentown, Pennsylvania, home, with its barn inspired timber frame great room and cupola, captured an Award of Excellence for its architect, K.W. Ramsey at the 2005 AIA Eastern Pennsylvania Design Awards Program. The timbers are Douglas fir.

The owners of this property wanted a home which looked and felt like a lodge. The great room is supported by four king post bents, while the adjoining gathering area is defined by a timber framed floor system. Exterior timber frame elements give a preview to what awaits inside. The timbers are Douglas fir. The general contractor and home designer was Stayco Construction, Inc. *Photographs courtesy of Dimitri Ganas.*

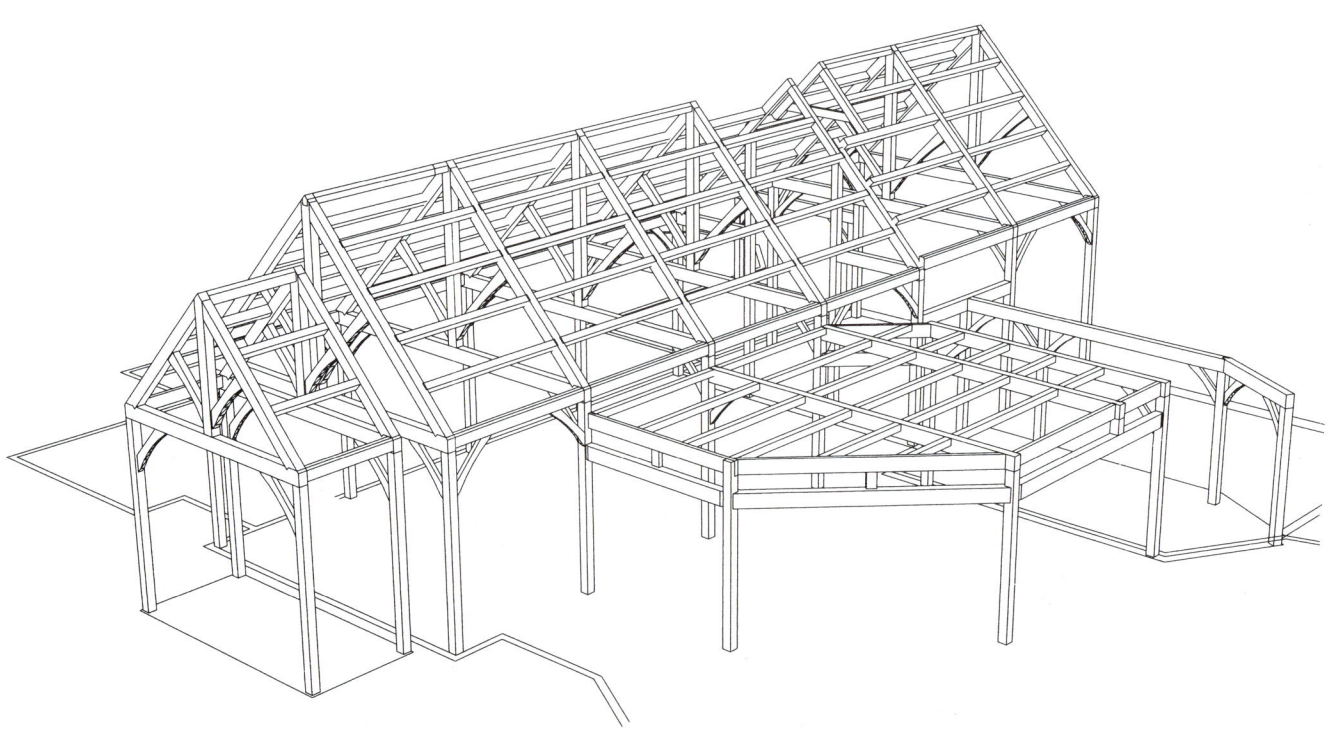

This Western Pennsylvania home has a number of exterior timber framed elements, as well as a timbered ceiling in the kitchen and dining areas, timbered rafters in the sunroom, and king post trusses in the great room. The timbers are Douglas fir. The house designer was Pippin Design. The owners acted as G.C.

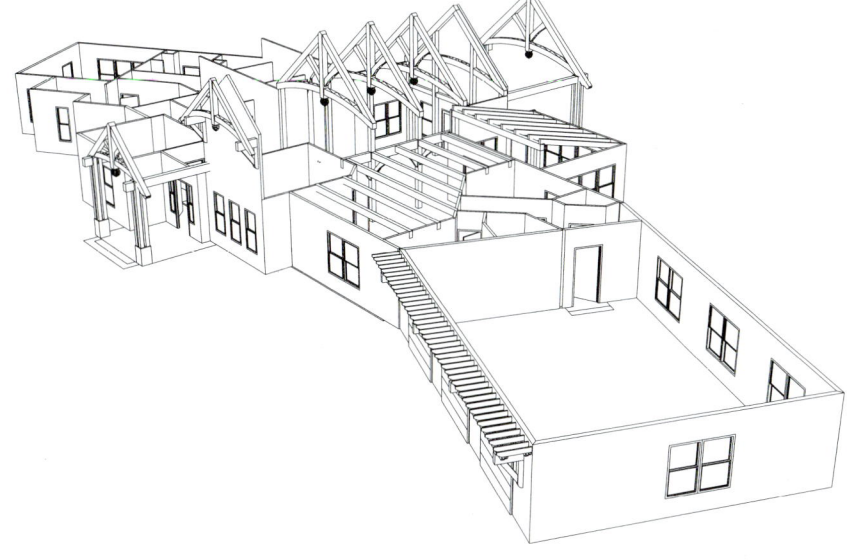

The timber framed areas of this Pennsylvania home include: the entrance, the great room, kitchen, dining, master suite, and porch. The Douglas fir timbers in the master suite are whitewashed, as are its ceiling boards. The house designer and G.C. was Wilson Enterprises, Inc.

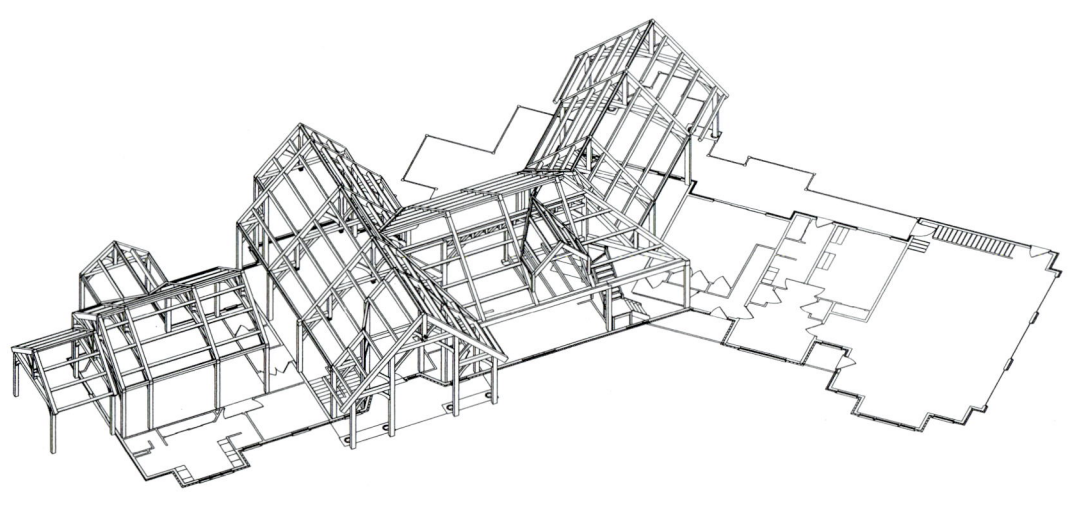

84

This simple king post truss system for this modest addition has an impact that exceeds its cost.

Two Douglas fir king post trusses and purlins sitting on conventionally framed walls support the roof of this in-home office addition.

Set on a lake front, this Virginia home has a timber framed great room with an office loft above. Timbers are Douglas fir.

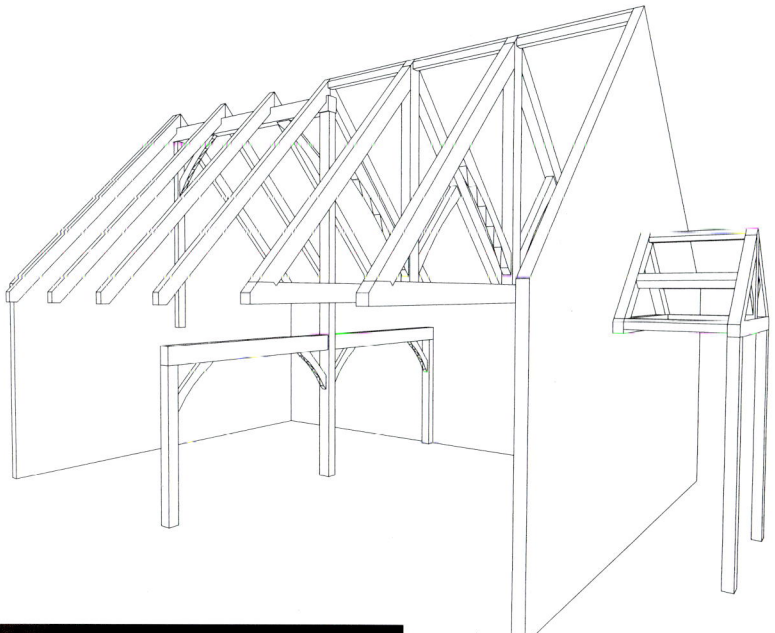

This Douglas fir trussed kitchen/dining room addition was to an old Maryland stone farm, a gable stone wall of which is visible at the kitchen end. An old stone cistern was located at the center of the room, and, rather than hiding it, the owners covered it with glass, half of which can be seen in front of the island. The G.C. was Bancroft Homes, Inc. and the architect was Archer & Buchanan Architecture, Ltd.

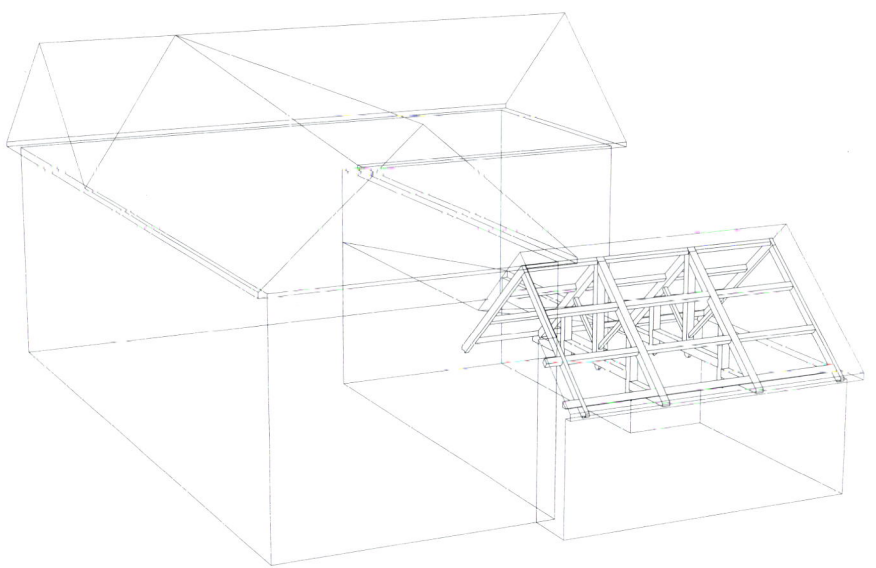

This Lititz, Pennsylvania, great room with scissors trusses set on conventionally framed walls was the first hybrid by the author. His client requested that the timbers be whitewashed and the ceiling material be gypsum wallboard. Zaya married her before the home was completed.

The owner/builder of this Lancaster County home wanted to incorporate some elements of a farm; hence the silo and barn inspired great room. The timbers are Douglas fir; the plank ceiling boards are poplar.

This Bucks County, Pennsylvania, home, designed and built by Casadonti Homes, Inc., showcases stained and varnished Douglas fir timbers. The great room was timber framed. Exterior framing elements give hints as to what is inside.

This two story 16' by 50' white oak addition to a Pennsylvania vacation home made the home so much more livable that the owners made it their year round residence. The architect was Kauffman-Hickey Architects; the G.C. was David McMillen Custom Contracting, Inc.

A one story red oak timber framed addition to this Allentown, Pennsylvania, home gave the owner the opportunity to display some of their cherished antiques. Concealed up-lighting along the plates warmly illuminates the ceiling.

97

The easternmost point of Long Island, New York, is home to the oldest (1658) cattle ranch in the country. When the owners, Rusty and Diane Leaver, discussed with Zaya their thoughts for a new home, the design path was readily clear. To help make the interior of the house feel like it belonged on the ranch, recycled (antique) timbers were integrated into the floor plan. The first floor is completely timber framed, while the second floor and attic above are conventionally framed. The planking used on the first floor ceiling is also recycled. Neither the timbers, nor the ceiling planks, were resurfaced, but rather used in their "found" condition.

One of the ceiling joists bears the initials of the person who first carved that timber along with the year it was pressed into service. Rusty & Diane acted as their own G.C. and did much of the construction work themselves.

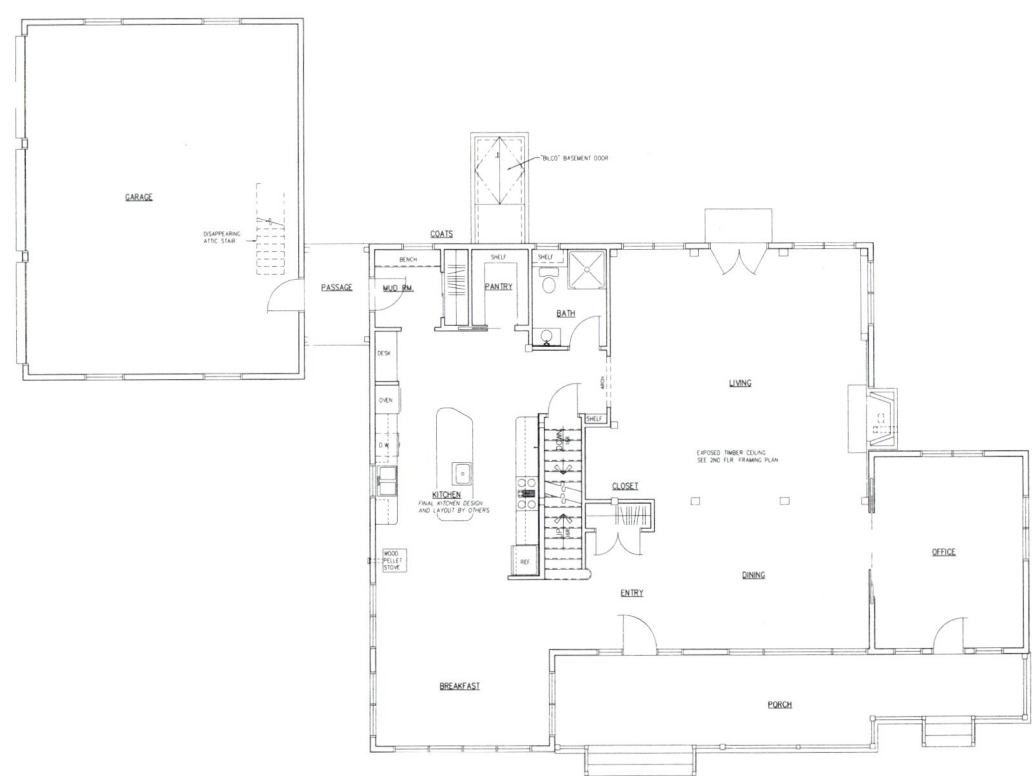

100

The center core of this Reading, Pennsylvania, home is timber framed with major purlins and a ridge supporting minor rafters. A catwalk connects second floor bedrooms at opposite sides of the timber frame. Timber joists tenoned on one end into a girt of the timber frame and set at the other end on a stick built wall form the ceiling of the kitchen. The timbers are Douglas fir.

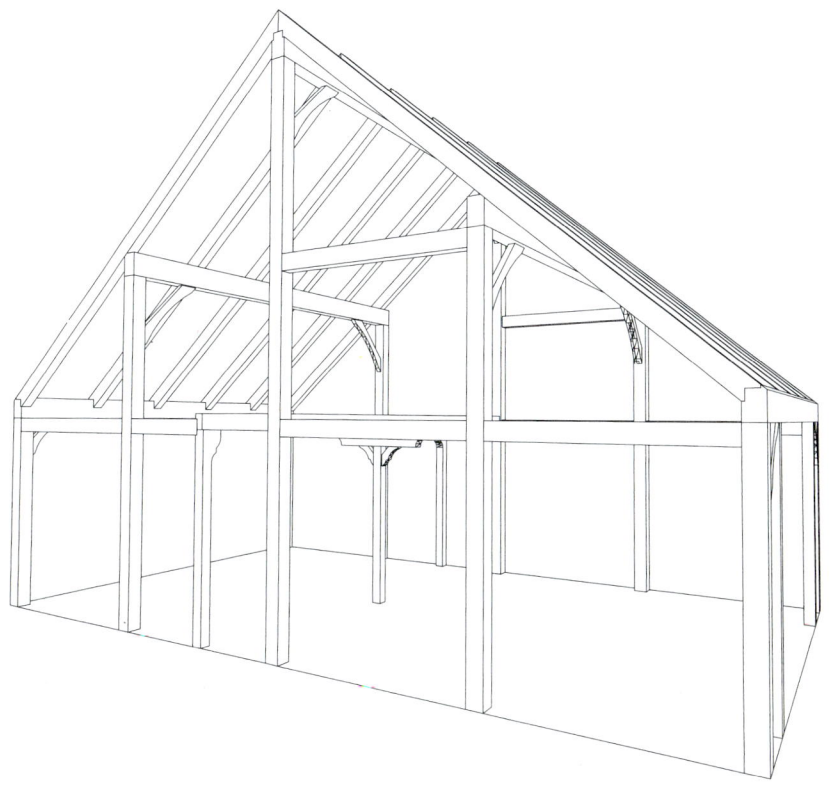

Recently completed, this Central New Jersey farmhouse is timber framed at its center core and at the wrap around porch. The timbers are white oak. The architect was Outerbridge/Morgan Architects, LLC.

This Southeastern Pennsylvania hybrid takes maximum advantage of a minimal numbers of timbers.

Three Douglas fir king post trusses tied to 2 x 6 walls support this Lancaster County, Pennsylvania, great room's roof.

This lakefront Pennsylvania home has a timber framed, prowed great room and timber joists in the kitchen, as well as the master bedroom. The timbers are Douglas fir. Often even simple embellishments can add drama to a structural element. Fairview Builders was the G.C. Residential design was by Lancaster County Timber Frames, Inc.

This Bucks County, Pennsylvania, kitchen addition, with its timber framed roof system, carries forward the feel of exposed ceiling beams used in the original house. The owner, Steve Swartley of Penn Builders, had worked with LCTF on a number of commercial projects but this project was his first use of timber framing in a residential project.

This almost completed Southampton, New York, spec house has a family room covered with three Douglas fir trusses joined together and into the gable end walls with purlins. A catwalk connecting second floor bedroom suites is integrated into the truss system. The architect was McDonough & Conroy Architects, P.C.; the builder/developer was KLH Building Corp.

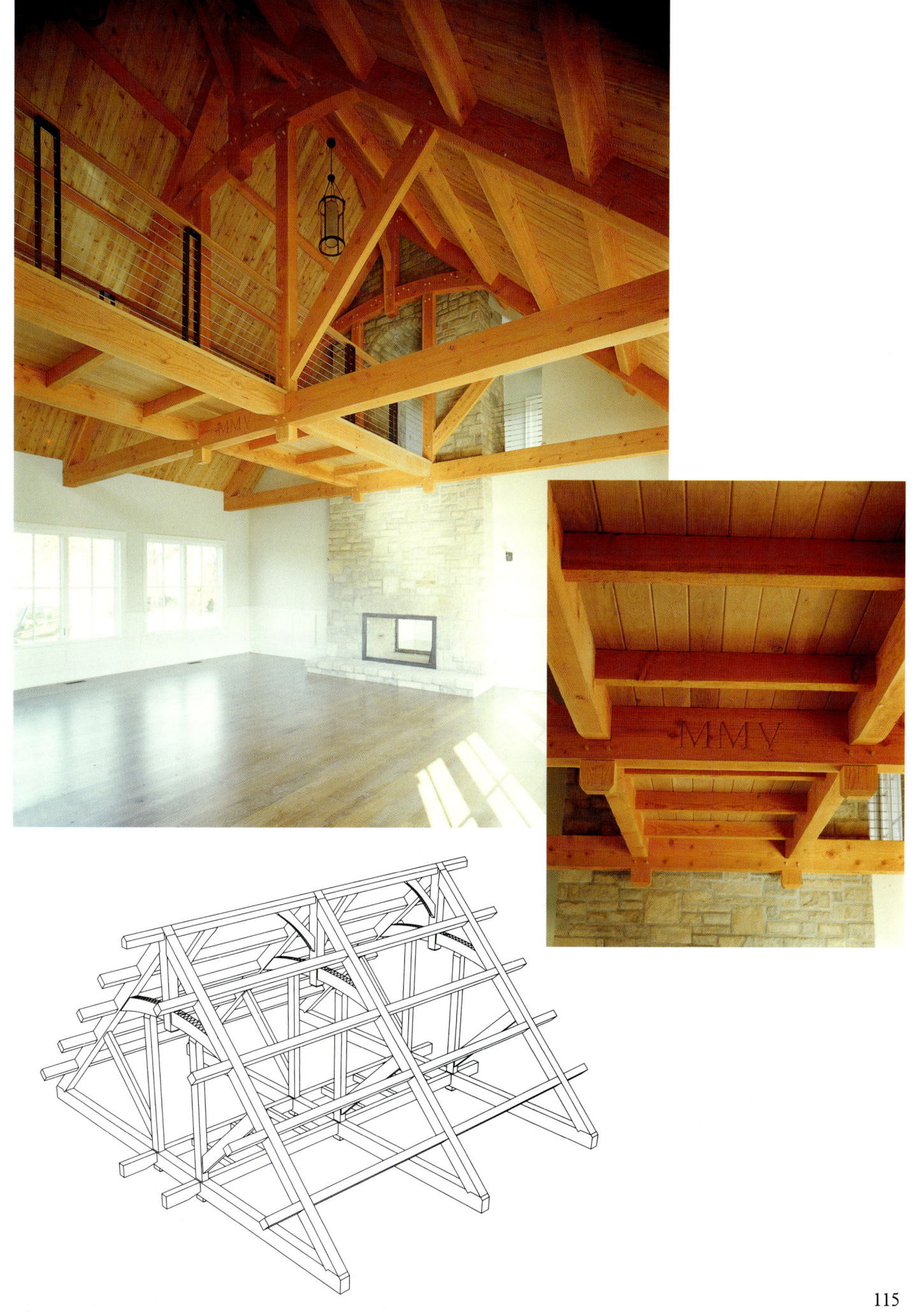

115

The king post trusses for this Westchester, New York, home were fashioned from recycled hemlock timbers harvested from a Pennsylvania barn. The lower chords were naturally arched and added a graceful aspect to the trusses. As a playful gesture, we positioned a "life like" bird into a hole gnawed by a rodent in decades past. The owners have left it in place.

This Southern Lancaster County, Pennsylvania, home has a Douglas fir timber framed great room with a queen post configuration, while the kitchen has a ceiling supported by summer beams and joists. The G.C. was J. L. Swope Construction.

Located in Western Ohio, this home employed a two king post truss system in the 24' x 30' great room and floor joists in the kitchen. The timbers are Douglas fir. The G.C. was Ben Baumer, Builder.

The 36' wide two story Douglas fir octagon of this "home nearing completion" in West Virginia frames the great room on the lower level and supports a walkway to living spaces at the second level. The G.C. was FMZ Construction & Development, Inc.

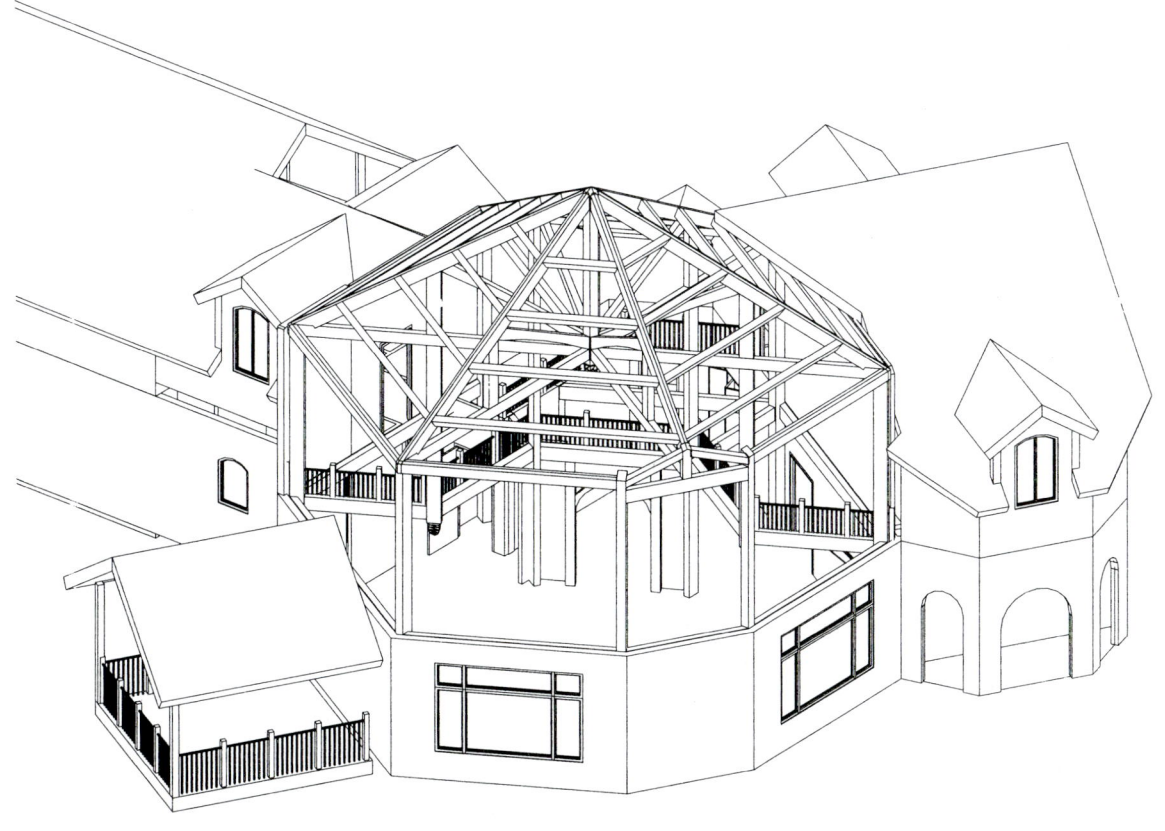

This Lancaster County, Pennsylvania, hybrid great room has two hammer beam trusses and one queen post partial bent that outlines the fireplace at the gable end wall. The timber-framed entry is stained grey. The timbers are Douglas fir. Elm Ridge Construction was both the G.C. and the house designer.

This Southampton, New York, spec house just nearing completion features a cedar timber framed porte cochere.

While neither this torii nor this barbeque pit structure are hybrids, we decided to include them to illustrate that even sparse timber framing can have a very dramatic impact.

This Lancaster County, Pennsylvania, home, built by Galen G. Miller, Inc. and designed by Wyant Architecture, has a low pitched Douglas fir and steel truss system with raised purlins, all of which gives the space a contemporary, industrial feel.

A historic Kennett Square, Pennsylvania, farm house and its closely situated rehabilitated barn were connected with a four bent, two storey timber frame. The large stone wall was the original end wall of the barn, linked to the original farm house by a bridge walkway of a single, 20 foot long slab of mahogany from pre-Castro Cuba. In the rehabilitated barn, modernistic steel and concrete construction is boldly married with the rugged timber framing of the original structure. The timbers are reclaimed and resurfaced white oak.

MAKING IT WORK

Hybrid Timber Frames and Truss Work

Timber frame hybrids have been built for millenia, combining heavy timber construction with a host of other building materials, from animal skins and mud loaves (known as "cob" to modern day practitioners), straw bales, wattle and daub, stone and other types of masonry to wooden wall boards, staves, and logs. Not surprisingly, most contemporary timber frame hybrids combine timber construction with the currently dominant conventional building methods – the ubiquitous "stick framing" or stud framing – and the rapidly expanding stress skin or structural insulating panel (SIP) construction.

Contemporary timber frame hybrids take a page from past building traditions and frequently apply timber construction where its structural function is clearest, and where it has the greatest visual impact – in the roof. After the first flush of traditional timber framing fervor had begun to subside, many timber framers of the last 25 years or so have applied their ingenuity to the integration of modern day conventional construction methods and timber framing – in a word, to the melding of two seemingly divergent philosophies.

As luck would have it, both stud and SIP construction are relatively easily adapted to timber framing. As a test case, let's have another, more detailed look at one of the hybrid timber frames in the previous section. Just about any one of them would work fine, but for the sake of simplicity, let's take the frame design shown in figure (1) and explore how this frame might be integrated with stud wall construction.

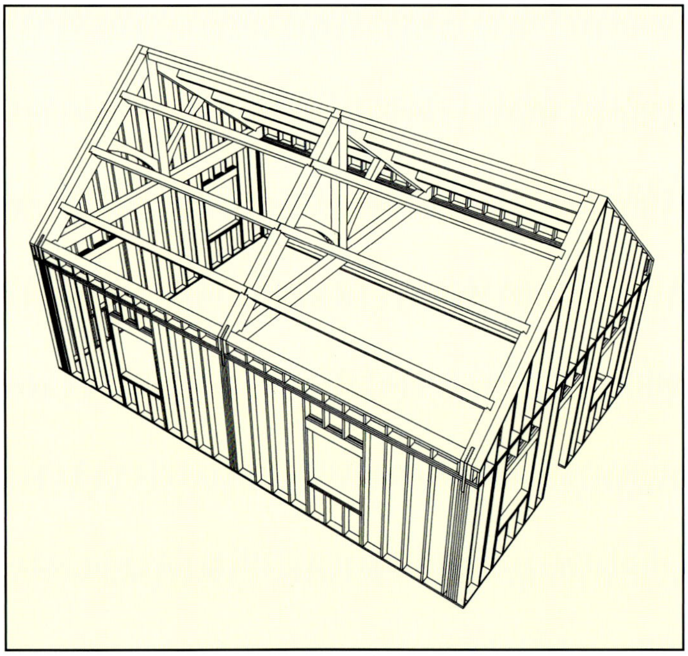

In a typical hybrid timber frame project, the general contractor – most probably not the timber framer – would build standard 2 x 6 walls up to the specified height to support the bottom chord of the trusses. At each point that the truss rests on the stud wall a post of ganged-up or nail-laminated 2 x 6 posts would be built into the stud wall to transfer the load of the truss and roof down to the foundation. This post could also be a wood composite material such as a Parallam™ or an LVL ("laminated veneer lumber") column. (See figure 2.) If the floor is conventionally framed with joists and plywood decking, solid wood blocking must be inserted below each of the post locations to make sure that the roof load is transmitted directly to the foundation and not just to the joists and deck.

If the frame does not include timber eave plates, then small "mini-walls" must be built up on top of the stud wall in order to provide support for the roof assembly at the eaves. (See the section below for a description of the "built up" roof assembly often used with timber frames.) This wall extension can be pre-fabricated and installed as soon as the timbers have been placed, or it can be built on site. In either case, the height of the mini wall should be adjusted to compensate for the probable shrinkage of the timbers. If the timbers were carved from green soft wood – such as Douglas fir – it's best to allow about 3/16" to 1/4" for shrinkage; with a green

Figure 1.

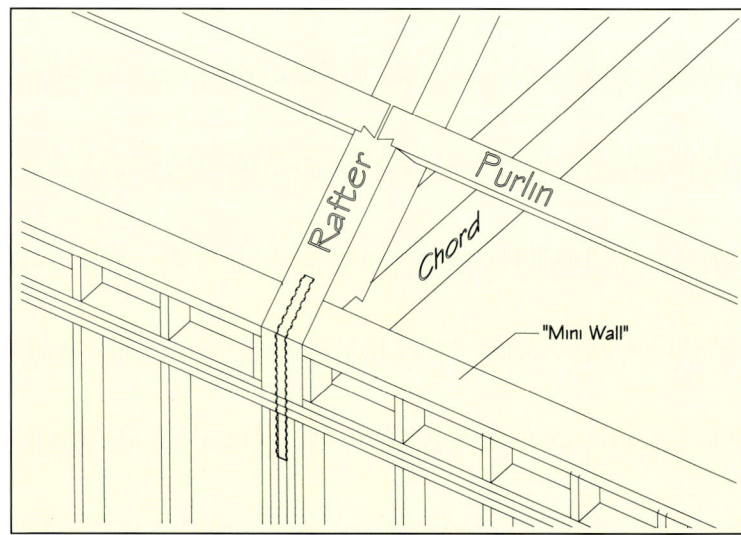

Figure 2.

hardwood – such as oak – 3/8" to 1/2" is a more prudent allowance. In the case of recycled or reclaimed timbers – such as those harvested from an old barn or factory building – the angled top plate of the knee wall can be set flush with the top of the principle rafters. Steel straps tie the timber trusses to the stud walls and counteract uplift on the roof generated during strong winds.

In our example the gable end trusses rest up against the stud-framed end walls. To ease the installation of interior finish wall materials such as gypsum wallboard, a furring strip – or "packing out" strip – approximately 1/8" thicker than the wall material should be nailed to the out-facing surface of the timber frame as in the drawing below. If 1/2" gypsum wall board is to be used, then 3" wide strips of 5/8" OSB (oriented strand board) should be nailed to the "out" surface (the back) of the timbers. This will create a groove behind the timber into which drywall or tongue and groove wallboards can be inserted. With this method, when the timbers begin to dry out and shrink, they'll simply pull back along the face of the wallboard, and won't pull away from the drywall, creating annoying gaps.

If, as suggested in the earlier section, you would prefer not to have the timber trusses placed up against the end walls – either because you would like to have window openings in that part of the wall or for reasons of greater economy – then the stud walls can be pressed into service supporting the timber frame purlins. (Figure 3.) The stud framing at the gable end walls will need to be modified to receive the purlins as in figure (4). The timber frame designer can provide an exact diagram showing the location of the pockets. They correspond exactly to the purlin dovetails on the principle rafters.

Often braces will be installed, either for structural reasons, or because the contribution they make to the appearance of the timber-framed room is desired. Their integration with the stud framing is handled in a manner similar to that of the purlins – pockets are created using the standard dimensional lumber of the stud walls. Figures (5) and (6) illustrate the framing of the stud walls and the creation of the pocket for the brace tenon. Interrupting the center stud at the correct height creates a mortise in the nail-laminated post to receive the brace tenon.

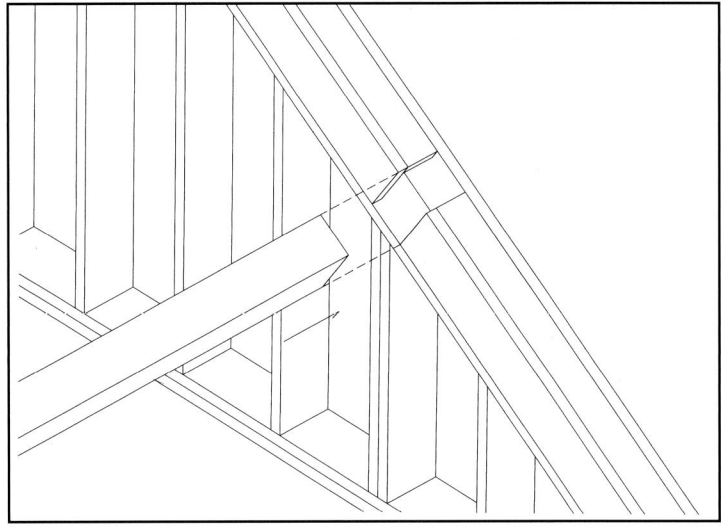

Figure 4.

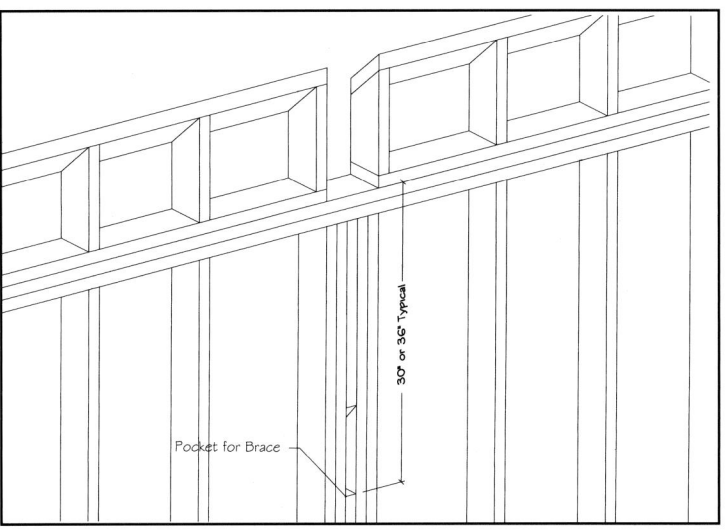

Figure 5.

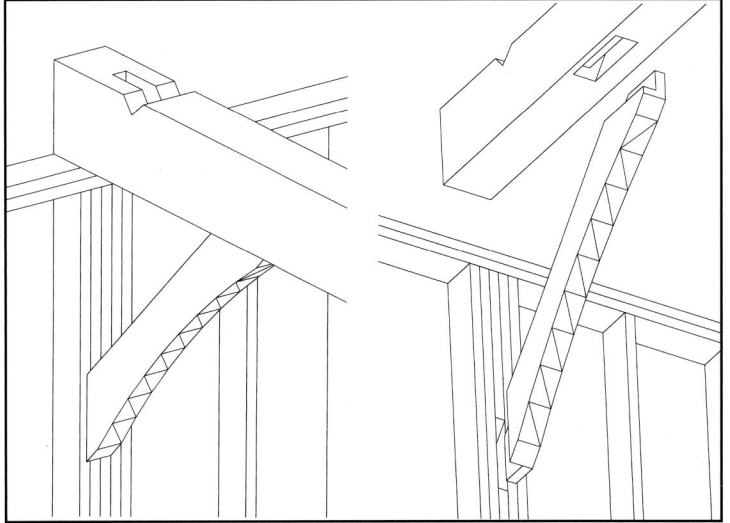

Figure 6.

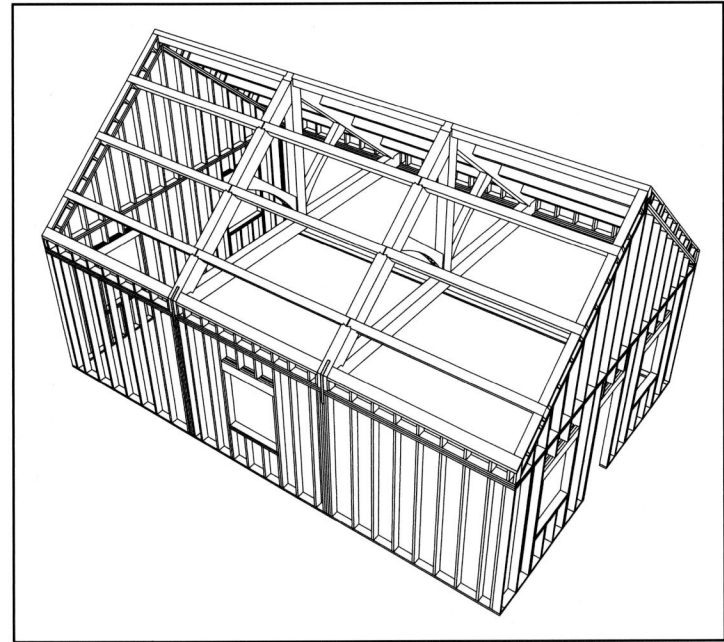

Figure 3.

When building with structural insulating panels rather than stud framing, the process of integrating the timber frame is somewhat different. Where the loads transferred to the SIPs from the timber structure are relatively slight (your structural engineer and SIP manufacturer will help determine what is permissible), the assembly method shown in figure (7) is generally adequate. The truss location dimensions are laid out on the surface of the SIP and sawn out. The next step is to remove the foam insulation to a depth of 1-1/2" on all sides where the 2 x 4 blocking attached to the timber are to be inserted into the SIP. The blocking attached to the timber should be of a width equal to that of the insulate layer in the SIP. They will provide surfaces to which the skins of the SIP are attached. Naturally, nails can be driven into the end grain of the timber to provide additional support. As in all SIP construction, joints should be carefully sealed with insulating foam to prevent air infiltration and condensation problems.

Often the loads transferred to the SIP require additional support. This can be accomplished by embedding a post of dimensional lumber inside the SIP as shown in figure (8). The panel joints should occur at the truss or timber load locations, with the foam insulation removed to the appropriate depth. Often a single 2x member is sufficient as shown here, but heavier loads can be handled by increasing the number of embedded studs and nail-laminating them as shown in the stud-framing examples shown above.

A similar approach is used when connecting purlins to panel walls. Again, the exact layout of the openings in the panel surface can be provided by the timber frame designer. Dimensional lumber is also used to provide attachment surfaces and to reinforce the openings made in the SIPs. (See figure 9)

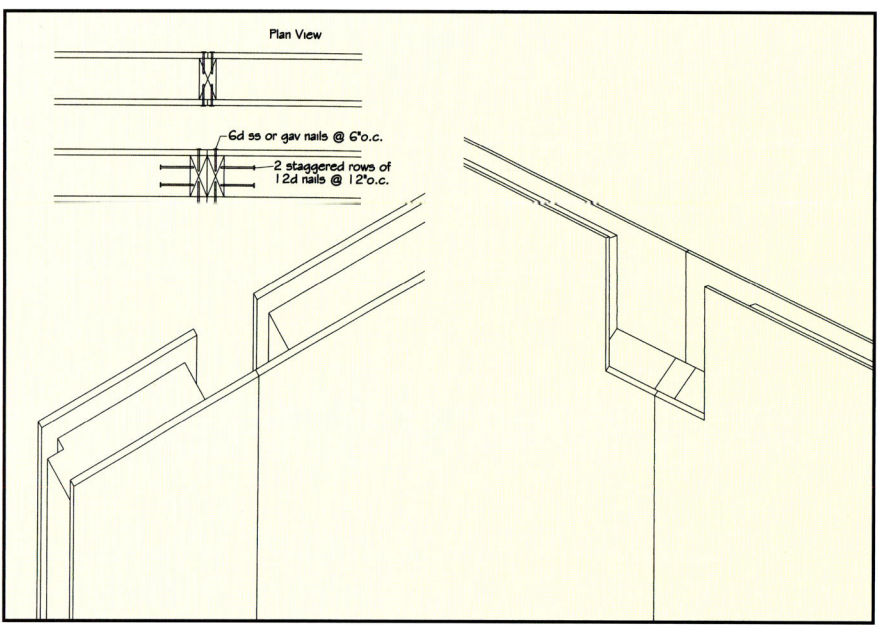

Figure 8.

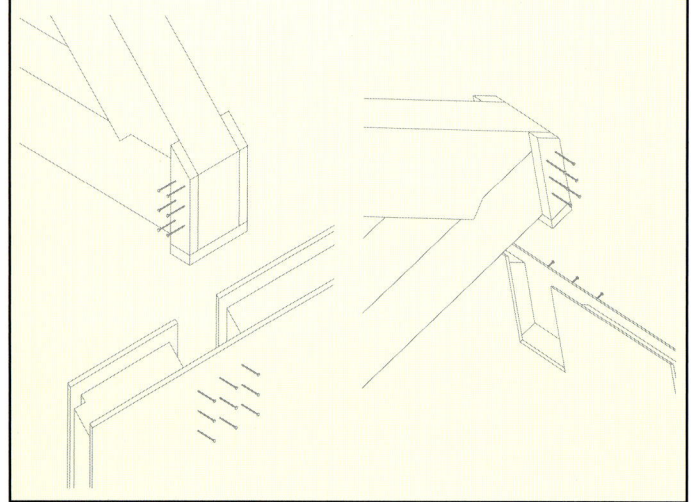

Figure 7.

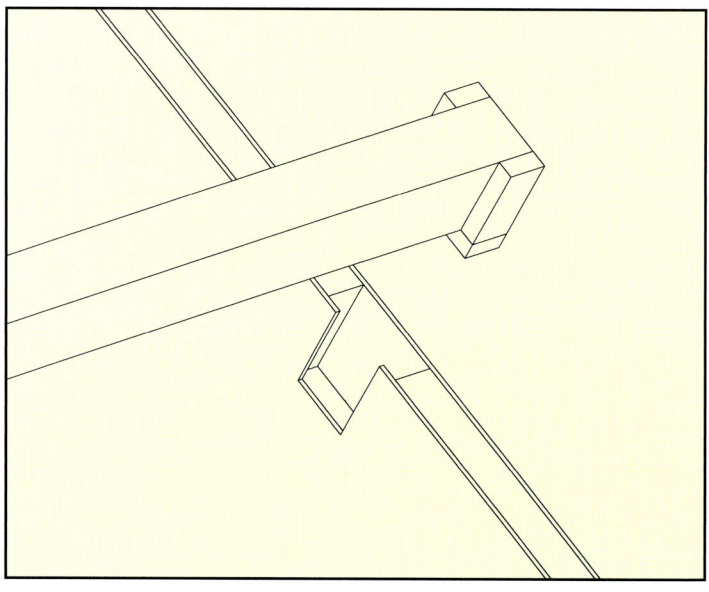

Figure 9. And here's a suggestion for connecting purlins to panel walls.

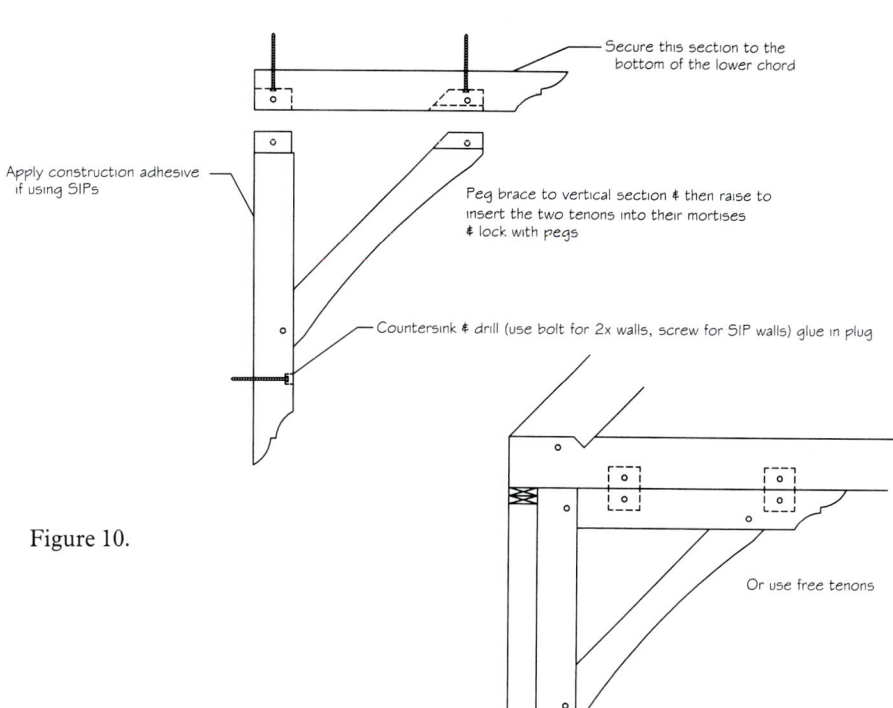

Figure 10.

Adding braces to a timber frame and SIP hybrid presents some challenges. It's highly impractical to create pockets for the tenon at the lower end of the brace, so using a bracketed brace assembly is usually the best solution. Of course, bracketed braces can easily be used with stud-framed construction, too, and are attached in much the same manner as to SIP walls. The installation methods detailed below will produce excellent results. (See figure 10)

Flat Ceilings

Without a doubt the room most likely to elicit a feeling of awe is the great room or main living space. Consequently, we've spent a lot of time on the truss and roof structures of timber frame hybrids, structures usually found in the great room. Besides the main gathering or great room of a timber-framed house, though, the atmosphere of other areas in a home can be greatly enhanced by the addition of timbers. These rooms might be the kitchen or dining areas, dens, bedrooms, or hallways leading to timbered spaces. Often these rooms will have a flat ceiling. If these ceilings are timbered, they, too, create an inviting feeling of depth and warmth. In some cases, a flat-timbered ceiling may be the only timber framing in a house. Because of the relatively simple joinery and lower material costs in flat ceiling timbers, it should come as no surprise that they represent the easiest and least expensive way to enjoy the warmth of timbered interiors. A few examples of the possibilities are described below, based on a rectangular room measuring 15 feet by 18 feet.

The simplest approach, of course, is to span across the width of the room with heavy joists. (See figures 11 and 12.) This arrangement is simple, clean, and straightfor-

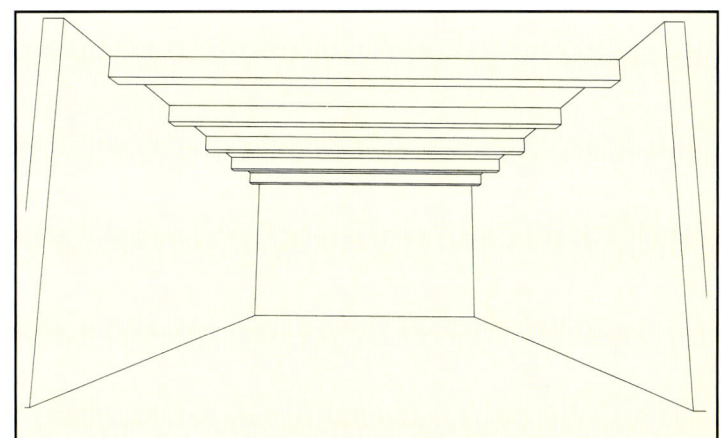

Figure 11.

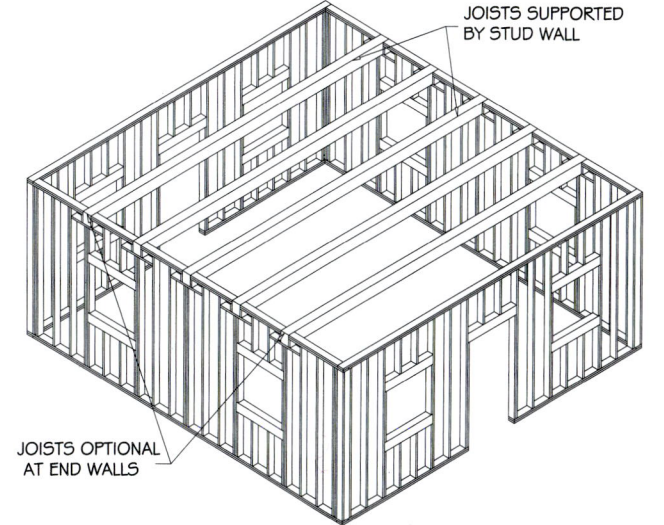

Figure 12.

139

ward. From the perspective of a framing contractor the installation of this type of ceiling could hardly be easier. The joists can land directly on and be fastened into the top plate of the wall, with the gaps between the top plate and the next floor or roof framing simply filled in with dimensional lumber. In the case of a SIP enclosure, pockets can be cut and blocked out just as we diagrammed for the purlin installation into SIP walls. Where the joists pass the plane of the wall stud framing one could rout a groove in them to receive the wallboard or other interior wall finishes. Using his technique, when the timbers begin to shrink as they dry, the shrinkage will be concealed inside the grooves. The problem of timber shrinkage can also be handled by attaching trim around all of the points where the timbers penetrate a finish material, but this technique can be pretty labor-intensive.

A simple approach may be what you're looking for, but if more timber is desired, either for structural reasons – as when there is a floor above – or for aesthetics, then a summerbeam can be added to span the narrower direction, with the floor or ceiling joists running perpendicular to it. A summerbeam is a heavy beam that divides the span of floor joists to increase the load they can carry and decrease the springiness of the floor above. (See figures 13 to 16) Traditionally, a summerbeam was usually wider than tall; that is, it appeared to lie on its side. It was also often supported by a post or two in the middle of their span, since it was intended to carry heavy loads.

Frequently seen in old barns and houses with second floor timber framing, summerbeams evoke the rustic side of timber framing. Contemporary timber frame designers will often incorporate them into a ceiling or floor design for this reason, even when the structural demands do not warrant such a heavy beam. One of the most appealing qualities of contemporary timber framing in its open display of the structural work being performed by the heavy timbers. Adding a second summerbeam – even when structural requirements don't call for it – emphasizes this quality, while referring to timber framing traditions. The joists and summerbeams of a flat ceiling can also be supplemented for visual and structural effect with posts and braces.

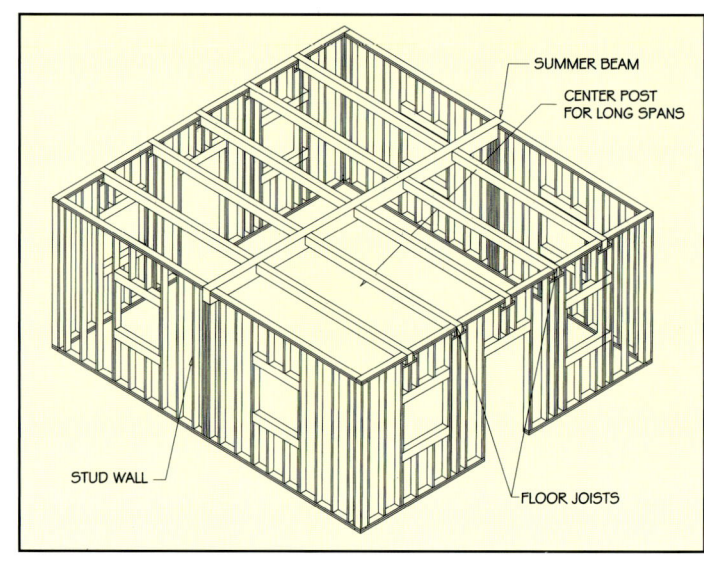

Figure 14.

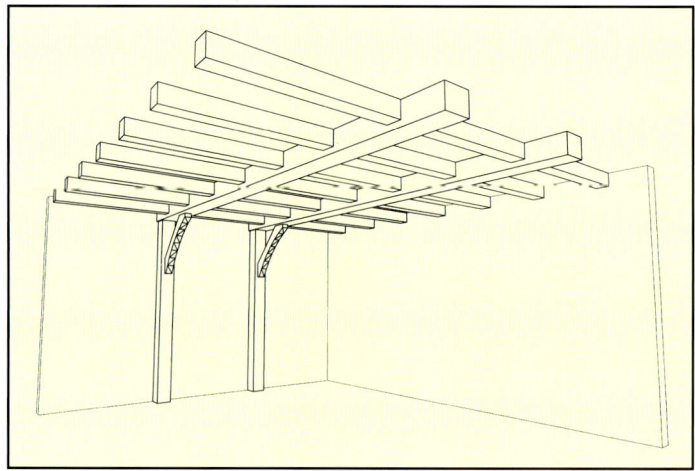

Figure 15.

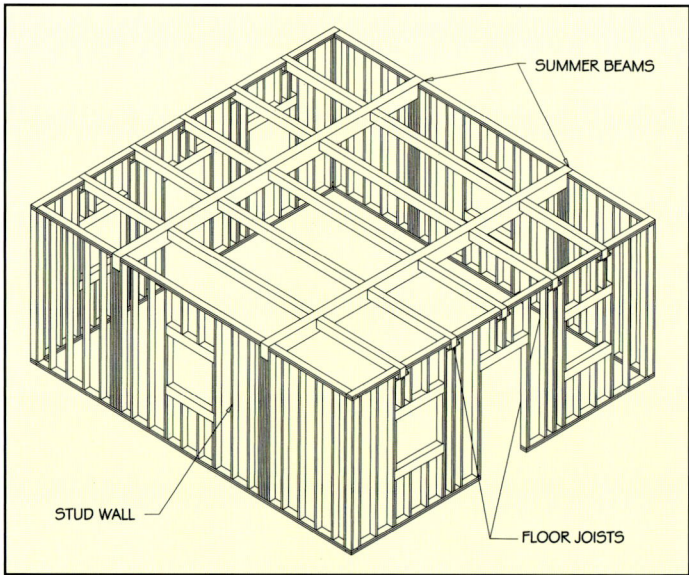

Figure 16.

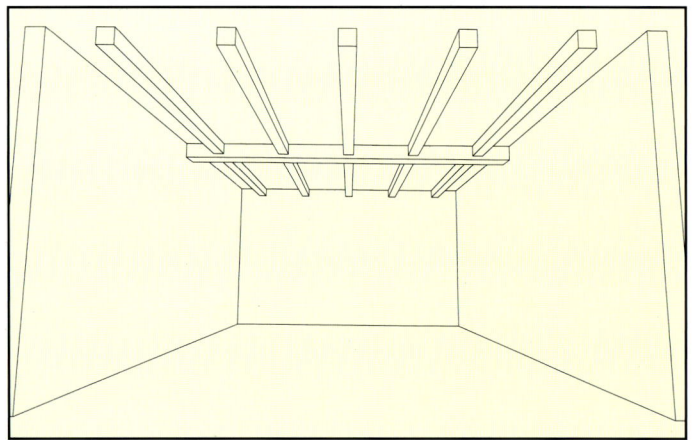

Figure 13.

Just what size timbers are used for the joists depends, of course, on the structural work they are being asked to do. Many ceiling and floor joists are 6 x 8 timbers, and, depending on the span, this size is usually adequate to carry some floor loading above. If there is no floor load, then a 6 x 6 or even smaller timber will often suffice. The charm of a timber frame relies partly on the mass of its timbers, though, so reducing their size down to the structural minimum can make the whole appear a bit spare. The spacing of ceiling joists is equally important, again, both from a structural as well as an aesthetic point of view.

Naturally, spacing the joists close together increases the load they can carry, in turn evoking their important structural function and intensifying the visual effect. In many situations a spacing of 48" from center to center of these joists will do the job structurally. This spacing would be a natural choice if one would prefer not to draw too much attention to the ceiling structure, or if one is concerned that greater timber density will feel oppressive. Particularly in a room with somewhat higher ceilings, spacing the joists 36" or 24" apart is the more popular choice. If the ceiling finish is to be gypsum board, the 24" spacing offers the added advantage of minimizing material waste by working with a dimension that divides evenly into the common 48" building module. Plaster board and other sheet goods come in 48" widths for this reason.

Whatever ceiling finish material is chosen – gypsum board, V-groove or square edge tongue and groove, even old barn boards – the installation will go much more smoothly if it can be executed from above rather than from below. Installing gypsum board from above, the panels can be cut to size, primed, partially painted, and screwed into position on top of the joists without having to secure them from below into 2x framing in the space above. Taping and spackling of gypsum board joints is held to a minimum this way. Wood furring strips at least as thick as the gypsum board are fastened to the top of the joists to keep the floor or roof loads from crushing the boards.

Installing wood ceiling boards from above offers similar advantages. The boards can be finished – oiled, pickled, stained, or varnished – and nailed into place on top of the joists. The use of furring strips to prevent crushing the plaster board would, of course, be unnecessary using wood ceiling boards.

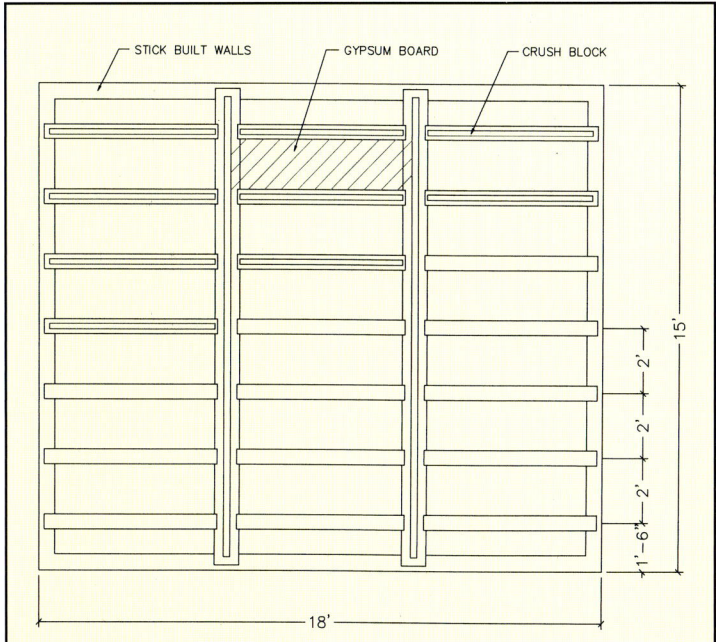

Figure 18.

A simple ceiling joist arrangement with plaster finish.
Photograph courtesy of Don Pearse Photographers, Inc.

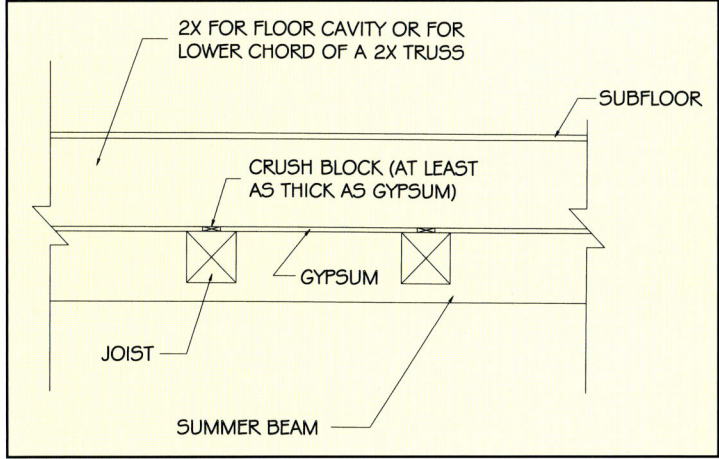

Figure 19.

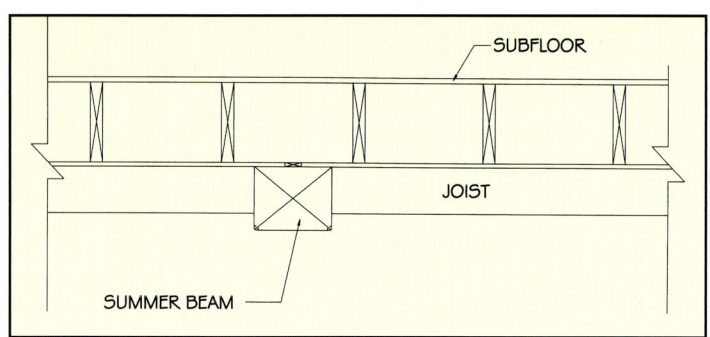

Figure 20.

There are times when it's impractical to install ceiling boards from above. Construction often has to proceed when weather conditions are less than optimal, and installing plasterboard on top of timber joists in even a light drizzle is certainly to be discouraged. Other construction particulars may make installation from above less desirable, and in these cases trim can be added to cover unsightly gaps between the timbers and the finish material. The trim should be attached to the timber so that it moves along with it when shrinkage begins to occur.

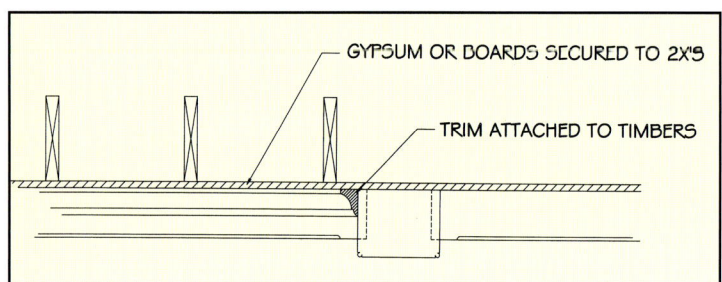

Figure 21.

Completing the Roof

The quintessence of shelter is the roof. Primitive shelter starts with structures that are all roof. Our earliest human ancestors are thought to have constructed lean-to type structures that favored the critical role of the roof. Much later, during the halcyon days of timber framing, the most important, and often the only, element of the frame was the roof structure. As we have seen, classical Egyptian, Greek and Roman building employed timber framing predominantly in roof structures. Certainly the timber roofs of the late medieval and High Renaissance cathedrals are a forceful illustration of the key importance of the roof structure, every bit as exalted an expression of the engineer's genius as the massive masonry walls, buttresses, and vaults.

The design of traditional Chinese and Japanese timber construction concentrated much of its ingenuity in the erection of a massive and complex framework capable of carrying the enormous weight of a ceramic tile roof, with relatively light construction in the walls. Even the construction sequence of traditional timber framed Japanese homes or temples illustrate the importance of the roof, proceeding from the erection of the posts to the roof timbers, and then directly to the roof covering. The construction of exterior walls, floors, and other interior features of the structure does not commence until a sheltering roof has been provided for them.

Throughout history and across cultures, the material that covers a timbered roof structure has always substantially determined the timber design and overall construction method. The situation is no different in contemporary timber framing. What covers the roof, how and when it is installed, how it is protected, and how it protects the timber framed structure and its occupants – these matters have been given considerable attention, and rightly so. Since the beginning of the timber frame revival in America a number of novel roof enclosure methods have evolved that are particularly well suited to the idiosyncrasies of heavy timber construction. One of these is the so-called "built-up" roof; another is the structural insulating panel (SIP) roof.

Either one of these enclosure methods begins with the material visible from the interior of the timber-framed room. In times past, when the timber frame was either hidden or tolerated due to lack of resources, that material often consisted of rough boards fastened to the timber rafters and purlins to serve as a substrate for the exterior roofing material. Honoring this early practice, the contemporary timber frame often employs tongue and groove boards, evoking feelings of anything from a rustic hunting lodge to a seaside cottage, from brooding, manorial austerity to sleek modernity.

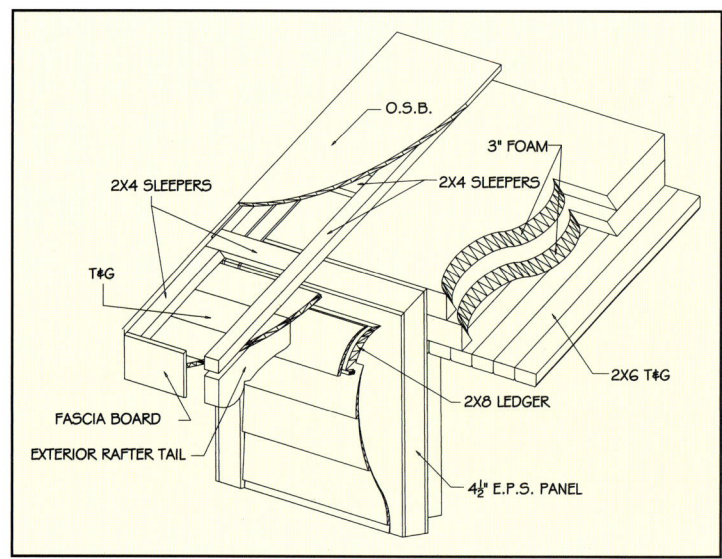

Figure 22.

A second common choice for the interior finish material is gypsum board. Though gypsum board is an invention of the twentieth century, other plastering and infill techniques have long been in use to "dress up," or finish, the appearance of timber frame enclosure materials. In contemporary timber frames, clients might choose gypsum board if they preferred to limit the "woodiness" of the interior spaces, or if they were looking for a brighter, airier feeling in the timber-framed spaces. Although plasterboard is less expensive than tongue and groove boards, it's much more labor-intensive finishing it out. It's rare that using it actually saves the homeowner enough money to justify its installation, so the best reason for the choice of plasterboard over tongue and groove is aesthetic preference. Doing as much as possible to finish the plaster boards before installation – especially in the case of flat ceilings – can help to minimize the extra labor costs. We'll have some installation tips below.

Aesthetic preferences aside, the big advantage of using tongue and groove instead of plasterboard is that, once it's in place and finished – it will never need any finishing again, whereas plasterboard will require periodic painting and other maintenance.

The dominant aesthetic of contemporary timber frames seems to lean in the direction of tongue and groove roof boards, so we'll focus mostly on an illustration of that material in what follows. Again, it may seem counterintuitive to install the roof boards immediately over top the finished timber frame, but this method can save the builder a host of aggravating and overly fussy work trying to fit boards in after the roof has been enclosed. The direction of the roof boards – parallel to the eaves and ridge versus perpendicular – is determined by the frame configuration. If it's a rafter system, the roof boards run longitudinally, parallel to the ridge beam; if a purlin system, the boards will run up from the eaves up to the ridge, vertically, as it were. In many cases, running the boards longitudinally will visually lengthen the timber-framed space; if the roof boards run perpendicular to the ridge, the vertical lines of the tongue and groove will convey a feeling of height.

Installation of tongue and groove roof boards.

Choices abound even with tongue and groove. It can be had in a variety of milled profiles and widths, of which v-grooved, beaded, and straight are the most common. If the frame is fabricated from recycled timbers, the choice of recycled boards might seem obvious. The v-grooved type creates highlights and shadows at every joint between the boards, emphasizing the linear quality of the ceiling surface. Beaded tongue and groove emphasizes this quality even more, and if the boards are beaded down the middle – and not just at the joints – the linear pattern becomes even denser. Straight boards – boards without any edge treatment – in contrast, tend to emphasize the expanse of the ceiling surface, drawing the eye more forcefully to the timbers themselves. Recycled boards enhance the rustic feel of a timber frame.

Tongue and groove roof boards can also be had in a range of wood species. In general, the species of the roof boards is chosen to contrast with that of the heavy timbers since using the same species for both can produce a monotonous effect. A common choice is white pine boards over Douglas fir timbers. The boards are often installed without any finishing treatment at all, or only a light oil finish, but the contrast between boards and timbers can be further enhanced by whitewashing. Of course, you might choose to have the roof boards varnished, imparting a gloss or satin sheen to the ceiling, an effect that can work well with carefully planned lighting. The least frequent choice of roof board finish is a darkening stain. The darker the stain, of course, the lower the ceiling will appear. In an area with a low, flat ceiling – such as a bedroom, kitchen, or dining room – this can become oppressive, so it is best to carefully consider this choice. Whatever the choice of finishes, however, it is almost always best to apply the finish before putting the boards on the frame. This makes the work of finishing much easier, avoiding labor-intensive measures such as taping off or cutting in, and eliminating the possibility of inadvertently spoiling the timbers. Be sure to treat the finished boards with care if you don't want footprints or other blemishes on your ceiling!

Roof boards or gypsum board are only the beginning of the roof system, though, and, in fact, their role may be strictly aesthetic. One popular method of handling the structural requirements of the roof is to cover them with structural insulating panels (SIPs). SIPs are often used as the enclosure system for the walls, but when used for a roof, they are usually thicker than those used for the walls because of the need for higher insulation properties (R-values, the resistance to heat flow through a material). Some companies supply SIPs with v-groove tongue and groove boards already applied to one side, but installing the roof boards on the frame discretely – before installing the SIPs – can often produce a cleaner look, allowing the installers to select and match the boards carefully for consistency and near perfect alignment.

For those who prefer the appearance of a plaster ceiling, SIPs are also available with "blueboard" already applied. (Blueboard is much like conventional plasterboard, but has a paper layer well suited to the application

143

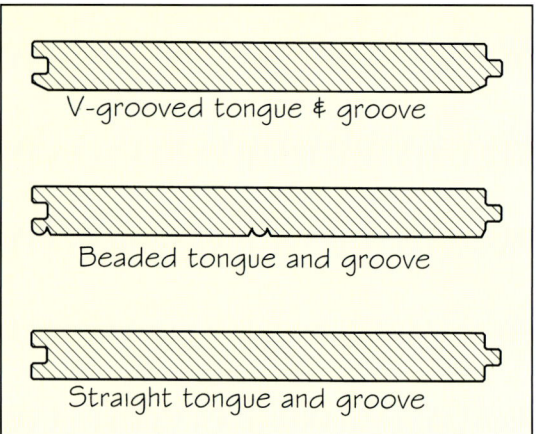

Figure 23.

of a specially formulated plaster skim coat.) Some panels (non-SIPs) are referred to as "curtain wall" panels – a single layer of oriented strand board, or OSB, adhered to the foam insulate with the blueboard on the opposite side. These panels are suitable for shorter spans, usually 4 feet or less. These work quite well with the typical purlin spacing of 4 feet on center.

If greater structural performance is required, a SIP comprised of two layers of OSB sandwiching the insulate and with the blueboard adhered to one side is the better choice. Either way, these panels are typically finished with plastering or painting after installation. With proper planning and layout, the seams between panels can land on purlins and rafters, greatly reducing the amount of plaster finishing required.

Structural insulating panels have many advantages, such as the speed with which the timber frame can be enclosed and protected; the structural integrity they lend the timber frame; and their excellent insulating properties. As one might expect, however, there are some disadvantages as well. They are difficult and often impossible to install without the services of a crane; there are additional costs to create a vented roof – a roof design that allows moisture and condensate to be vented away from the roof materials; the installation of finish roofing materials requires the perforation of the outer skin with attachment hardware; and some finish roofing manufacturers consider the SIP's 1/2" thick OSB stress skins to be too thin for their roofing products. If cost is no object, ordering custom-made SIPs or adding a second layer of sheathing over top of the SIP can solve this problem.

Another method of enclosing the roof that overcomes these shortcomings is the so-called "built up" roof. As one might expect, this type of roof is ***built up*** of several different roofing components, one layer at a time. The built up roof generally begins with the installation of roof boards, just as one might do with a SIP roof. (Installing gypsum board in place of tongue and groove requires special measures, which can't be detailed here.) A barrier of either traditional roofing felt or of synthetic composition is then installed atop the boards.

Now come the sheets of rigid foam insulate. The foam insulate comes in sheets of varying thicknesses usually measuring 4' x 8'. The most common thickness is 3", but 1", 2", & 4" thick sheets are also available. Different combinations of thicknesses can be assembled to meet varying insulation requirements of a particular region.

The sheets are made of either extruded polystyrene or urethane, the latter having the higher R-value. Generally, two layers of this insulate are spread out on the roof plane, with the second layer offset from the first to avoid "stacking" the seams between sheets. The insulate is held in place by 2 x 4s fastened with long screws or ring shank nails through the foam and roof boards into the purlins or rafters of the timber frame. These "sleepers" are laid with the 3-1/2" face down at a spacing of 24" on center, and are left "wild" – or overlong – at the eaves to help with the creation of the overhang, fascia, and soffit. Once this build up is complete, the overlong sleepers can be trimmed to length for the overhang, and the framing of the overhang can commence, to be followed by the installation of the finish roofing substrate, typically 5/8" thick CDX plywood. From this point forward, the completion of the roof proceeds as in any other roofing operation.

The 2 x 4 sleepers create a 1-1/2" space between the insulation and the plywood roofing substrate which can be used to vent condensate and heat from the eaves up to the ridge. This contributes to the life of the roof. Also, the materials are small and light enough to maneuver up onto the roof without a crane. Finally, this system is easier and agreeably less costly than achieving a vented roof system with a SIP roof.

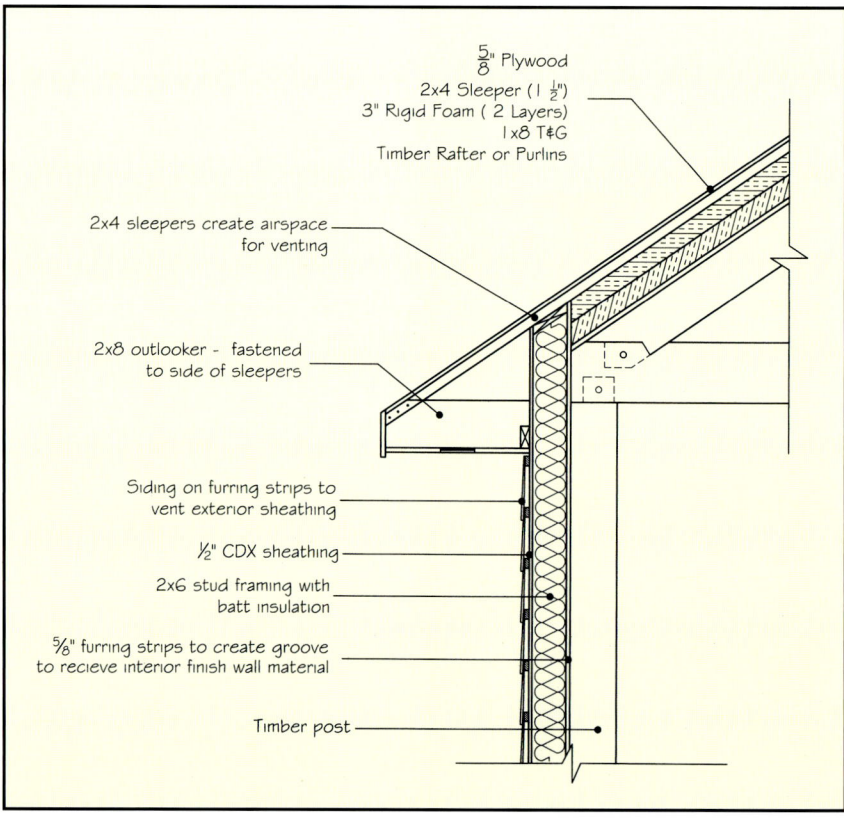

Figure 24.

THE PROCESS

After the timber framing drawings have been completed and sealed, one person assigns each timber its position in the frame and lays out the joinery and cutting details on each piece. Another person will follow behind to check and verify each line and mark on each timber. After he signs the pieces, the artisans begin the carving operations. As each piece is completed, the artisan carving that timber initials each and every joint. After all the pieces have been carved, the frame is fit together in a two-dimensional plane and bored for the pegs which will lock the frame together at its final site. Then, each piece is edge treated according to the type chosen by the clients, followed by the sanding and hand finishing.

After the finish is dry, the timbers are stacked and covered in another building until the shipping date. At the building site, the timbers are offloaded and staged according to the sequence in which they will be raised. Some timbers are raised individually; others are joined together before being lifted into position by the crane. It is desirable to get the roof and sidewalls on as quickly as possible after the frame is complete.

The frame shown here is the central core of the house. Two conventionally built wings will complete the structure.

In our company, the men who erect the frame at the site are the ones who carved it at the shop. To all of them, it is the high point of the whole process – sort of the culminating experience. More than one of the men keeps a photo album of each frame they have carved and raised.

Using a chain mortiser to cut mortises.

Laying out the timbers.

Hand chiseling housings.

Pre-fitting the carved members.

Drilling peg holes in the pre-fit frame.

Sanding timbers prior to oiling or staining.

147

Assembling timbers on the ground on the day of the raising.

Picking the assembled truss.

Truss being flown over the waiting posts.

Lowering the truss onto the post tenons.

Setting a ridge beam.

Setting the sunroom girts.

The finished frame with the roof boards installed.

ADDITIONAL CONSIDERATIONS

"The whole is greater than the sum of its parts." For this statement to be true, each part is to be treated as important, if not critical, in establishing that whole. So as consequential as is the shape and configuration of the timbers and as influential as is the background surface – be it gypsum, plaster, or wood – the additional choices that must be made, including species, surface texture, edge treatments, and finish of the timbers, are also weighty; and, therefore, are to be considered carefully.

The selection of species and the grade within that species has a huge impact on the appearance of a frame. Broadly speaking, smaller and fewer knots, straighter grain, and fewer and shorter checks ("cracks") are the criteria that define a more "perfect" timber species and grade. Some people view such timbers as "boring looking," while others would view such timbers as clean and subtle.

If you are in the former group, look to oak; if you are in the latter group, look to Douglas fir in at least a grade of Select Structural FOHC (Free of Heart Center). Some people like the natural tint of fir; others like the color of white pine. Aesthetic considerations aside, species indigenous to your area will be less expensive. But with hybrids, you will be using less board footage than with a whole house frame, so this factor will be less of a constraint.

Surface Texture

Wood, more than any other structural material, invites touching, if not caressing. Both visual and tactile senses demand satisfaction from a timber frame. Following are examples of some of the surface textures available. On a practical note, smooth surfaces are easier to dust.

Planed and sanded Douglas fir.

Circular-sawn Douglas fir.

Band-sawn Douglas fir.

Reclaimed rough-sawn timber with a hint of whitewash.

Reclaimed hand-hewn oak showing mortise and peg holes.

Reclaimed hand-hewn oak.

Douglas fir timber curve-planed.

Edge Profiles

The edges of a timber may be left as is; with curve-planed or hewn timbers, they almost always are. With rough sawn timbers, a slight radius is common; a stop chamfer (by a saw, not a router) is not uncommon. Historically, heavy rough sawn posts in factories were deeply stop-chamfered. Eliminating the edges greatly enhances the fire resistance of timbers.

Smooth timbers almost always have some sort of edge profiling, with the most popular being the stop chamfer. Profiling the edges has some decided practical advantages: splintering and denting – a possibility even in the harder species – become much less of a problem. The are aesthetic advantages too: a heavy timber can be given more grace since a dressed edge eliminates some of the visual weight of a timber and the more intricate edge profiles, such as a beaded edge, can add a shadow and impart more formality.

It is not an all or nothing situation. A good practice is to vary the intensity or size of the edge treatment depending on the size of the timber. Massive timbers warrant a pronounced edge treatment. Also, there are no rules that preclude mixing types of edges on the same frame; in fact, this can often be done to good advantage. We have had excellent results employing beaded edges on horizontal timbers, while putting stop chamfers on all the other timbers.

Standard stop chamfer.

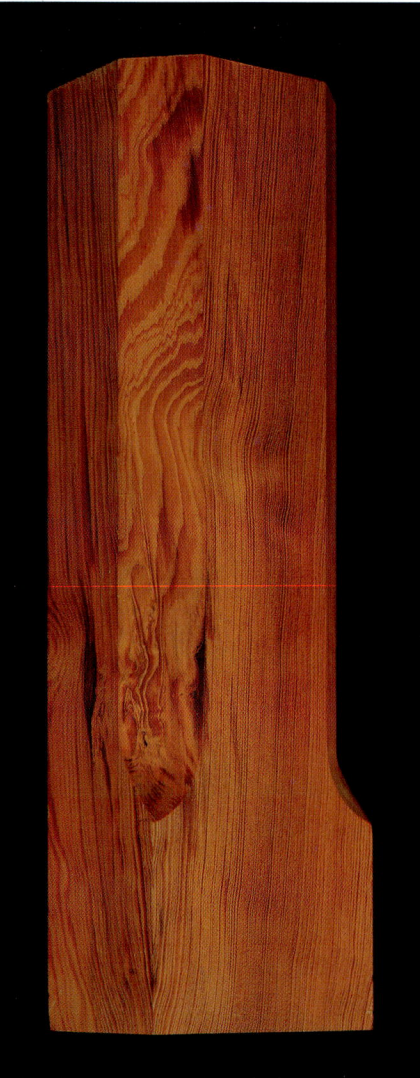

Heavy stop chamfer on recycled Southern yellow pine.

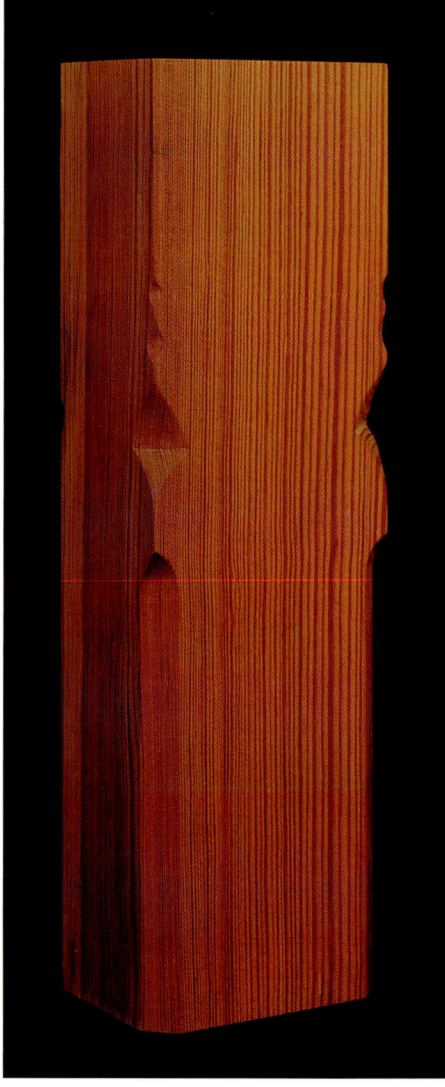

Standard stop chamfer with lamb's tongue detail on recycled Southern yellow pine.

Finishes

The most popular, and perhaps the most efficient, finish for interior timbers is a clear oil. The oil enriches the wood, slightly darkens it, and makes it look natural. Dirty fingerprints and smudges clean up easily.

Some clients opt for whitewashing the frame. This process yields excellent results if the goal is to add lightness and subtlety.

Staining interior timbers a dark color is, in our opinion, almost always a bad decision. Dark staining is basically an attempt to mimic the look of an old frame. It is a poor attempt. Time will darken most interior timber and Mother Nature does it best. If dark timbers are desired, reclaimed members from an old factory or barn, while costing more than stained timbers will look infinitely better. Another downside to dark staining is that scratches or nicks cannot be easily repaired. With stained timbers, the whole face would need to be re-sanded and re-stained. Also, dark stain, applied before the timbers are well seasoned (which is usually the case), will cause any check that opens to be incredibly pronounced. The darker the stain, the more pronounced the open check.

Exterior timbers, if untreated and not maintained, will change in color rather quickly. Grey is the usual result. If that look is not desired, there are several options available, none of which are once and done. Painting the timbers offers the best exterior protection and can be a highly effective design choice.

Cove edge rout on recycled Southern yellow pine.

Beaded edge rout on recycled Southern yellow pine.

Tung oil finish on Douglas fir.

Golden oak stain on Douglas fir.

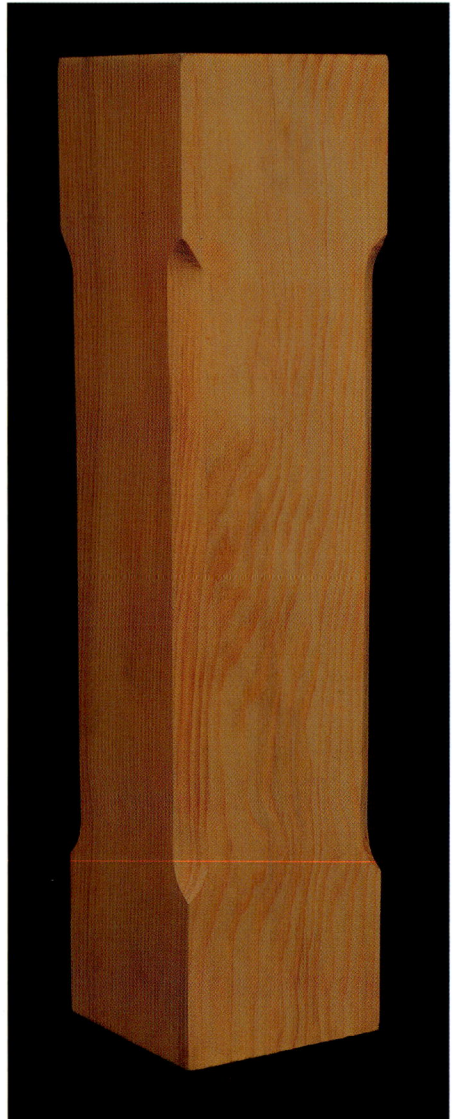
Tung oil finish on Douglas fir.

Golden oak stain on Douglas fir.

Medium dark stain on Douglas fir.

Dark stain on Douglas fir. Whitewashed Douglas fir. Whitewashed reclaimed rough-sawn oak.

A FINAL NOTE

Our intentions, in writing and compiling this book, were to show that:

1) The history of the timber frame hybrid is pretty much the history of timber framing.

2) Our affinity for, and attraction to, heavy wooden timbers is so much a part of the human experience that it is hard-wired into our psyches and long ago crossed geographic and cultural lines.

3) Structure can, and perhaps should, be sculpture—or stated differently, materials can be fashioned to inspire as well as protect.

4) The possibilities for judiciously and selectively incorporating timber framing into our lives are boundless.

5) Limiting the areas of the home that are timber framed reduces costs, saves natural resources, and intensifies the appreciation of those timbers that are used.

Hopefully, we have not fallen too short of these intentions.

The opportunity to participate in the design of one's own personal environment doesn't come to everyone. And, perhaps it shouldn't. Those who dislike making decisions, those who never learned to defer gratification, or those who place little or no weight on the creative process are usually better off and less challenged by simply buying or renting a home that was designed and produced for general consumption. Those of you who are excited and passionate about directing the form of your new environment are about to embark on a thrilling and fulfilling adventure. We hope we have helped.

POSTSCRIPT

I think that I shall never see a poem as lovely as a tree.
–Joyce Kilmer

This solitary white oak forms a canopy of over 100 feet. It stands at the edge of Zaya's property within sight of the office where Lancaster County Timber Frames was founded. This sentinel has been ravaged by the gypsy moth invasion of the 1980s; it has taken numerous shocks from blinding, angry bolts of lighting; and it has been assaulted by thick, tenacious vines. It has suffered droughts and has felt gale force winds.

Yet it has prevailed, and still continues to grow. Its fullness has been cleft and its shape twisted. Nevertheless, maybe because of this, this tree continues to inspire us to do justice to those trees that have been harvested so that we may practice our craft.

BIBLIOGRAPHY

Adam, Jean Pierre. *Roman Building, Materials and Techniques*. London: Routledge, 2005.

Affolter, Heinrich Christoph, Alfred von Känel, and Hans-Rudolf Egli. *Die Bauernhäuser des Kantons Bern*. Basel, Switzerland: Schweizerische Gesellschaft für Volkskunde, 1990.

Benson, Tedd. *The Timber Frame Home*. Newtown, Connecticut: The Taunton Press, 1988.

Brandon, Raphael and J. Arthur. *The Open Timber Roofs of the Middle Ages*. Ontario, Canada: Algrove Publishing Limited, 1999.

Chapell, Steve. *A Timber Framer's Workshop*. West Brownfield, Maine: Fox Maple Press, Inc., 2005.

Chinese Academy of Architecture. *Ancient Chinese Architecture*. Beijing, China: Building Industry Press, 1982.

de Camp, L. Sprague. *The Ancient Engineers*. New York: Barnes & Noble, 1993.

Hoffsummer, Patrick, et al. *Les Charpentes du XIe au XIXe Siécle, Typologie et évolution en France fu Nord et en Belgique*. Paris, France: Editions du Patrimoine, 2002.

Fu Xinian. *Chinese Architecture*. New Haven, Connecticut: Yale University Press, 2002.

Guilt, Joseph. *The Encyclopedia of Architecture, The Classic 1867 Edition*. New York: Crown Publishers, Inc., 1982.

Heavrin, Charles A. *The Axe and Man*. Mendham, New Jersey: The Astragal Press, 1998.

Hewett, Cecil A. *English Historic Carpentry*. Fresno, California: Linden Publishing, 1980.

Higham, Robert and Philip Barker. *Timber Castles*. Mechanicsburg, Pennsylvania: Stackpole Books, 1995.

Izenour, George C. *Roofed Theaters of Classical Antiquity*. New Haven, Connecticut: Yale Press, 1992.

Pryce, Will. *Buildings in Wood: The History and Traditions of Architecture's Oldest Building Material*. New York: Rizzoli International Publications, Inc., 2005.

Sandstrom, Gosta E. *Man The Builder*. New York: McGraw-Hill Book Company, 1970.

Ssu-Ch'eng, Liang. *Chinese Architecture, A Pictorial History*. New York: Dover Publications, Inc., 2005.